MAKING the Journey

MAKING *the* Journey

Katrina Marti

from Mormonism to Biblical Christianity

For more information or to purchase additional copies visit:
www.thejourneymormonismtochristianity.blogspot.com
ISBN 978-0-615-53429-9

Printed in the USA

Publishing consulting and production: Aimazing Publishing & Marcom, Phoenix, AZ, www.bonniesbooks.com

Dedication

I dedicate this book
to those who helped me see the truth,
to those whose eyes are being opened,
and most of all, to Him who gave me true
and abundant life—the Lord Jesus Christ.

Table of Contents

BEEN THERE, DONE THAT

"Been there, done that; got the T-shirt" is a common expression people make when they've experienced similar things as you have, but they don't really want you to continue talking about those things. Well, that's not exactly the sentiment I'm trying to express. However, in the most literal way, it is. I've been there and done that, and used to have the garments to prove it. As a result, I do know where you are and where you've been. Plus, I've experienced many of the same frustrations, fears, and confusion you're experiencing now.

I've seen the confused look on a Christian's face when I've asked, "What about the priesthood?" I've received the garbled answer when I asked my pastor why I had to "walk the aisle" to show what Jesus had done for me. Actually, you don't—it was a tradition in that particular church. I've sat in a worship service and thought how irreverent people were by clapping, raising their hands, and more. I've wondered how anyone could ever feel the Spirit with that upbeat praise music. I've watched and listened to Christians pray; then I hoped and prayed that no one would ever want me to do that. You see, I've done all that and much, much more. I've also felt the absolute and utter aloneness that comes from being the only ex-Mormon in a Christian gathering, having no "roots" to rely on, and no sense of "Christian" traditions that mirror the rest of the worshippers. I've felt the pain as Christians called the religion my family holds dear "a cult," "crazy," "weird," and more. I've had people tell me that they don't see how "any intelligent person" would ever join "that" church.

Because I've been there, I hope I can help you in a very real and very practical way. I hope that I can help you wade through all the "junk" that's out there outside of Mormonism. I hope I can help you see what the Bible teaches about all the important issues. At the same time, I want to provide a clear perspective into biblical Christianity to help you figure out some of what it's all about.

So, where do I start?

My family on my mom's side has been LDS since nearly the beginning of Mormonism. They knew Joseph Smith personally. I have at least one great-great-grandmother, or she might have been my great-great-great, who saw Brigham Young when he "took on him the mantle of Joseph." Many generations back, Brigham Young asked a great-grandfather of mine to wait at Winter Quarters and farm for a few years so that others could resupply when they arrived. Being obedient, he did just that, until Brigham Young gave him permission to migrate to the Utah Valley several years later. He and his family settled in Springville Utah, just south of Provo.

Another of my greats came across with the Martin Handcart Company and nearly lost her feet in the cold. Another great-grandmother was a sister wife in polygamy and suffered a lot of hardship after her husband effectively abandoned her after the Manifesto. She found great comfort serving in the Manti Temple. At one point in church history, the temple listed her husband among the men who "owned" it, so that the federal government could not take it over.

So, on Mom's side of the family, I come from a long and rich family history of very active LDS church involvement. My dad was a convert and was baptized when I was eight years old. However, because of his inability to give up coffee and smoking, his degree of active involvement in the church fluctuated. Even then, to this very day, he too holds the church to be true and is staking his life and his eternal destiny on that fact.

I grew up in the church and loved it. I'm a very social person and found all my social outlets in the church. When I was a child, my mom would pack our Volkswagen "Bug" full of children, literally up to ten children in that little car, and we'd head off to Primary every week. Those were the days before the seat belt laws took effect. Because my mom was Primary president and then Junior Sunday School president, and my dad was Sunday School president, we were heavily involved in all those activities.

As I grew into my teen years, we moved, and once again I was surrounded by a wonderful group of friends and supportive adults. My friends' parents became aunts and uncles to me, and I love them dearly to this day. Every Saturday night, my friends and I attended Stake Dances, and we spent one week every summer at girls' camp. In general, church activities consumed my entire social life. And I loved everything about it—from the solemn trips to the temple for baptisms for the dead to the boisterous nights at girls' camp; from the teasing looks we gave each other at testimony meeting where we would challenge one another, "you go first and then I'll go," to the root beer socials where we tried to suck up homemade root beer with a plastic pipe from a clean garbage barrel. Okay, I admit it; that wasn't my favorite activity.

As I approached adulthood, however, I fell away from the church. The honest truth is that the church and all it represented just didn't fit into my life at that point. Even then, I believed it was a wonderful organization. I visited the Salt Lake Temple Visitors' Center whenever I went to Utah, rolled down the hill at Manti with my kids, and participated in Visiting Teaching whenever they tracked me down and made attempts to reactivate me. I received other visiting teachers with enjoyment, a bit of guilt, and remained a "Jack" Mormon—guilty, but not guilty enough to do anything about it.

When my oldest son was eleven years old, I experienced something that would change my life forever. It started innocently enough; he asked me if he could be baptized. I suspected Grandma had been coaching him. So, at that time, I started taking him to church. If you were over eight years old, before you were baptized you had to take the missionary discussions. Since my son was eleven, we had to follow that rule. Honestly, I didn't want to do all this. It was a hard time in my life: there was trouble in my marriage; I was unsettled in my career; in general, church didn't fit in with my plans. Nevertheless, I went and began the reactivation process. It actually wasn't that hard because I knew the routine pretty well—buy the boys some white shirts and ties, get myself a dress, and start going. Some things had changed a bit, such as when and how they did Primary. For the most part, however, it was the same old routine. There were still three meetings in a row on Sunday, kids' activities once a month, and then all the home obligations such as Family Home Evening and reading the Book of Mormon.

After attending church for several weeks, I had a spiritual experience—a life-changing experience. I can't explain it very well, but perhaps the best description is that God reached down and gave me a bear hug. The love and joy I felt was truly amazing. I realized that I had been longing for God's love in my life for so many years. In fact, it was bigger and better than anything I could have imagined. It filled a hole in me that I had known was there, but I didn't think could be filled. I also knew that I had to make a decision: to live for God and continue to experience that fullness, or to continue to live my life as I had been living it. It sounds like it should have been an easy decision, but it wasn't. It truly was a giving up of self—of my own right to rule myself. It was about letting God make the decisions in my life by submitting to His holy, infinite greatness, as opposed to doing it myself. It involved admitting that I was living sinfully, and that it separated me from God. I had done things that were offensive to Him and I needed forgiveness.

I agonized over this decision. My "self" desperately wanted to stay in control, even if my own self-rule wasn't exactly perfect or particularly bringing me happiness. Finally, after much agonizing and soul-searching, I gave in to God and gave my life up to Him.

Let me add a disclaimer here for those who are already biblical Christians reading this account. At that point in my life, I had unbiblical ideas about who God was, who Jesus was, who I was, and what God wanted from me. Some might believe that theologically speaking, I couldn't have been saved, but the bottom line is that God was working in me even through this first, life-changing encounter with Him. He continued to be faithful, and will continue to be faithful, in preparing me for something even greater.

Shortly thereafter, I returned to full and complete membership in the LDS church. I started attending full-time, and practically every single activity I could. I was the super achiever—on fire for the church and for God. I went through the temple and got my endowments, always paid a full tithe, and accepted callings. I taught the four-year-olds in Primary and wrote a Ward newsletter. Later, I taught Sunday School to twelve- and thirteen-year-olds and worked in the Young Women's Organization. I attended every single meeting I could. Once again, I loved the church. The people were friendly, and my social life revolved around church once more. My friends were clean, moral, worked hard, and loved their families.

During this period, I also developed a passion to learn everything I could about the church. I reasoned, sensibly, that because the church was true, it surely would hold up to scrutiny. Therefore, I set out to discover just what it taught from every source I could. First and foremost, I chose the standard works. I read through the Book of Mormon in only a few days; then I settled down to read some again, each and every day. I read it with my boys as well. We actually completed it together once. Of course, I read the Bible, Doctrine and Covenants, and Pearl of Great Price also.

In my personal life, however, I faced more challenging issues. My marriage fell apart, and it was an extremely difficult time for me. Only a short while later, I met my current husband, Steve. Steve, too, had come from a generational LDS family and had been very active in the church for the first thirty-five years of his life. However, he left when his doubts got too big for him.

When I met Steve, God was doing a work in his life. Steve actually got rebaptized shortly after we started dating, although that would ultimately turn out to be a mistake. Being the very committed LDS person I was, and holding full confidence that the church was true, I was absolutely confident that God would manifest the truth of the church to Steve and that we'd soon be married in the temple for eternity. In short, Steve and I married, and we started down the path that I was sure was heading to eternal happiness.

One month after we were married, however, Steve confessed to me that he was once again having some doubts about the church. This new revelation presented quite a difficult challenge for us.

We were newly married; we were dealing with my rebellious teenage son; and we were now divided in our religious life. Through it all, I held to my belief that the church was true—and with all my heart, I believed it was. I had faith that Steve would come around to see the truth. He was too sincere a seeker not to see that eventually. Honestly, more than anything else, I trusted in God. I didn't understand Him as I do now, but I did know that He, and He alone, was faithful and would be faithful to bring us together religiously.

As we continued to talk, study, learn, and grow, I secretly observed Steve. I watched his wholehearted sincerity in seeking the truth. I watched him study the Bible to gain more knowledge about God and serve Him in all he did—even outside the church—something I had truly thought impossible. I watched Steve spend hours on his knees begging God for a testimony of whether the church was true. I watched also as he fasted for weeks in order to know God's will for our lives.

Finally, after we'd been married about a year and a half, God spoke very clearly to me and told me that when Steve made up his mind, I should follow. Knowing the covenants I had made in the temple, and knowing a little bit about what the Bible taught, I didn't think this was contrary to what God would want. I agreed to do just that. Of course, all the while I assumed Steve would decide for the church. I was so sure this was God's will that I even told Steve about it. That conversation made him even more determined to make the right decision because he knew it would now affect all of us.

Several months later, Steve did make up his mind. To my surprise, however, his decision was to leave the Mormon Church. Still, I was confident that God would help him see the truth. I optimistically assumed this was a detour that God was leading us on. In due course, we'd see, without a shadow of a doubt, the truth of His church—the LDS one, of course.

As a result, I went to my bishop and told him my decision. I handed in my temple recommend and walked away, fully expecting to return after a short while. In my heart of hearts, I was still very much an LDS person.

The first Sunday after the big decision was interesting. Now I can see how God's hand was on us every step of the way, but then I just thought that any church would do. Because our infant daughter was up half the night, the church with the latest service was the one we chose. That church happened to be a small Southern Baptist one in my hometown. Honestly, I was scared to death. I knew someone was going to jump out and scream at me, or preach to me, or . . . I don't know really what I expected, but for sure it wasn't going to be good.

Nothing out of the ordinary happened; except, I met a woman named Sue whom I had known in college several years before. Although I didn't know her very well, her life exhibited as a kind, true, and committed Christian. She was someone I could respect and trust, which took away much of my fear of "those Baptists." Sue invited me to a ladies' Bible study at the church on Wednesday mornings, which also happened to be my day off from work.

I started attending that study and found the ladies there to be very nice. They introduced me to their style of Bible study, which admittedly was a bit different from what I was used to. They had a book they were following, and each lady should have read the chapter or chapters in the book for that week. They would show a short video from the author talking about that week's chapter. Afterward, the ladies would discuss what they had read and finally, after the study, they'd pray for each other. Their manner of prayer was also quite different. They'd first ask if anyone had a prayer request; then, one by one, they would share problems in their lives, or in the lives of friends or loved ones, sometimes being quite open and honest about sin issues, anger issues, and other very personal concerns they had.

After everyone had the chance to share, the ladies would just start praying outloud, individually, as they felt like it. There was no external pressure on me to pray; except, of course, that I thought I should. I found it a very strange way to pray, but comforting also.

I continued to immerse myself in studying the Bible. I really did want to know what it said about, well, everything. Having no lack of determination, I started reading only my Bible and keeping track of certain things I wanted to learn more about. I became even more curious about the nature of God, who Jesus was, the priesthood, the Word of Wisdom, and so forth. I started a notebook and I wrote down every single instance when any of those topics came up in my reading. Eventually I got around to compiling that work and doing what I called a "thesis." Steve was just finishing his master's degree, and he put no more time into his thesis than I put into my compilation, hence the name.

Interestingly enough, and to my great surprise, my Bible studying led me away from the LDS church and not toward it. Within six months of attending the ladies' Bible study and tenaciously studying even more on my own, I found myself really and truly out of the LDS church—heart and soul.

The journey, however, wasn't so very easy. In fact, it was hard. It was probably the hardest thing I've ever done. For me, to make the transition to biblical Christianity from Mormonism was to turn my back on my friends, my upbringing, my heritage, my pride, and nearly everything in my life up to that point. It was saying I was wrong to my kids, who didn't believe me for a while. It was saying I was wrong to my coworkers, my mother, and even to my ex-husband, who had told me I was wrong all along— ouch! In addition, it was relearning practically everything I'd ever known or learned about God, who He is, what He wanted from me, and even what was truly right and wrong, including things I'd learned from the time I was a baby. It was also risking rejection by my family, my friends, and others I truly cared about. In some cases, these were people who in many ways were nearer to me than my family. It was telling them I thought they were wrong and then dealing with the consequences in our friendship as a result. It was losing the security of knowing I was in the one true church, knowing its routines and patterns, as well as the ebbs and flows of life in that church. It was literally a step of faith off the cliff of the known into the unknown.

I have to say now, though, being on the other side of the journey, that it was all worth it—100 percent worth it. God was faithful to lead and guide me and be there with me every step of the way. And the joy and peace I found in knowing Him—the biblical Him, has no comparison to the difficulty of the journey.

Are you there? Are you ready to step off that precipice into the unknown? Probably your journey to this point looks different from mine. Maybe what bothers you is the church's history of polygamy, or maybe the character of Joseph Smith, or the way the modern prophets keep changing history to fit what they want you to believe. Maybe someone in the church truly offended you, which caused you to start questioning some other things, which brought you here. Or maybe like me, you've been reading the

Bible, and it's just not adding up with what you've been taught your whole life. If so, then this book is for you. My hope and desire is to help you make that transition—to look at and investigate biblical Christianity and find out what it's all about, and to explain biblical Christianity to you, so that you can do your own investigation and either accept or reject what I've learned.

You may, in fact, think you know quite a bit about biblical Christianity. If you do, then great! I hope I can answer some of your questions as an outsider about the craziness of Christianity. In the process, I hope I can also answer some of the questions that most, if not all of us who've left the church, have asked ourselves. For instance, if this church isn't true, which one is? What about priesthood authority? How do I choose a church? What about that crazy idea of the trinity? Which Bible is the true Bible? Can I really trust the Bible? And more.

Most of all, I hope I can encourage you that our God is big enough to handle all your fears, doubts, troubles, insecurities, and even temper tantrums. I know, because He's taken on mine and handled them quite well, as well as those of many I've mentored. Despite the battle, despite the loss of relationships with LDS members, family members, and dear friends, and despite the uncertainty and fear we've experienced, every single one of us is glad that we've made the transition. The cost is high—but the prize is much, much better than anything we could ever imagine.

Introduction
TO MY NEVER-LDS CHRISTIAN FRIENDS

I so appreciate your support of me in writing this book, and in financially supporting its printing and distribution. I truly believe this book can and will be used by God in reaching those who are in the midst of leaving the LDS church and in helping them make the transition to biblical Christianity. As your sister in Christ, and partner in this endeavor, I can't say enough about how wonderful it is to be part of your family, and to praise and worship our Lord and Savior Jesus Christ beside you.

Friends of mine are missionaries to a very remote tribal group in a third-world country. Not only did my friends spend years getting to know the language of the tribal group, but also they spent years trying to understand the tribe's worldview.

Despite the years this process took, my friends felt their time was well spent because, when they started to teach the gospel to the tribal people, they were able to communicate in a way that addressed the tribe's fears, assumptions, and presuppositions. Because of this, the people were able to understand the gospel clearly without the barriers of cultural differences that are so present in ministering cross-culturally. In many ways, my friends spent years learning to think like the tribal people.

This book is very much like that, except that I don't have to spend years learning about the underlying assumptions of Mormonism—I've lived it. And, like my missionary friends, my point in writing this book isn't to help Christians understand Mormons better, but instead it is to speak to Mormons in their heart language, and within their worldview. For this reason, this book is written specifically to your Mormon friend, and designed to address their underlying worldview, fears, assumptions, and pre-suppositions in their language. I hope you'll support me in that. For this reason, though, you may even see some areas in this book that you wonder why I wrote in that particular way. It's because I'm speaking Mormonese, and not Christianese. What I mean by this is that we, too, have a language we speak: Christianese, if you will. In this book, I've purposely avoided (or tried, anyway) speaking Christianese. The reason I've done that is that our Mormon friends also use the same words we do, yet they mean something entirely different.

I've also had some friends suggest that a book explaining Mormonism to Christians would be helpful to them, and I agree. However, in my looking at books in this genre I've found that there are plenty of great books that do just that. *Speaking the Truth in Love to Mormons* by Pastor Mark J. Cares is a great example of a book that talks not only about LDS beliefs, but also about the Mormon culture. *One Nation Under Gods* by Richard Abanes is another great resource that looks at Mormon history. Ron Rhodes, Bill McKeever, and Donna Morley are some of the other authors whose books grace my shelves. And there are many, many other books that talk about Mormonism and explain their basic beliefs to Christians. The Institute for Religious Research is a great organization, and I can wholeheartedly recommend their online resources as up-to-date, loving, and compassionate.

In the end, though, I believe there is a very real need for a book that talks specifically to Mormons in the language they speak and from their point of view to explain to them what the Bible teaches and why. And that's what I've attempted to do in this book. I hope you'll stand with me, pray with me, and even be able to share this book with the Mormons in your life who are in the midst of transitioning out of Mormonism and into biblical Christianity.

Finally, I just want to say thank you all over again: it's you guys who showed me the way to know, really know, my Lord and Savior Jesus Christ. It's you guys who showed me, through your lives, what the Christian life looks like, and it's you guys that God is going to use in your Mormon friends' lives most powerfully, and often without words. I love you guys!

A NOTE TO MY LDS FRIENDS ON
HOW TO USE THIS BOOK

My friends,

My deepest desire is that this book can be a blessing to you. I recognize that the concepts in this book are more than just huge; they are life-changing. Honestly, you might not be ready for everything it teaches. There might be some chapters, which no matter how well I wrote them, you aren't going to understand. These might even make you mad or, at best, uncomfortable.

The bottom line is that the search for truth is not always easy, and more so when we've been taught something well, as we were in the LDS Church. I hope, though, that I can reassure you that God is very interested in the truth. In fact, truth is His business. Check out what the scriptures have to say about Him:

> The LORD, the LORD God,…abundant in… truth…. (Exodus 34:6-7)
>
> For thy mercy is great unto the heavens, and thy truth unto the clouds. (Psalms 57:10, 108:4)
>
> …I will cure them, and will reveal unto them…truth. (Jeremiah 33:6)
>
> …and the truth of the LORD endureth forever…. (Psalms 117:2)
>
> And ye shall know the truth, and the truth shall make you free. (John 8:32)
>
> Jesus saith unto him, "I am the…truth…." (John 14:6)

Because God is very, very interested in you knowing Him, He's going to teach you about the real and truthful Him, even at the cost of you having to give up what you've always held to be true. It surely happened to me, and to most ex-Mormons I know. In fact, it's happened so many times to me that I sometimes think my Christian walk is a series of admitting to the Lord that I was wrong about this and about that, and then letting Him correct me. So in case you're like me, instead of throwing this book in the garbage when you hit one of those spots that you really can't accept, or believe what I've written, just set it aside.

In fact, what I'd suggest is that you do set it aside. However, don't set aside the study for truth; instead, pick up your Bible and start the search for truth yourself.

One suggestion I make early on is that you get yourself a notebook. As you read through your Bible, start taking notes. Make notes of those things you just can't reconcile with yourself and your worldview. The trinity is a big stumbling block for many of us ex-Mormons. It is a good example of something for you to start studying on your own. Whatever the issue is that you're saying right now "I'll never accept _____," start writing down what it is, and what God has to say about that issue.

As far as this book goes, read the things that help you now. When you finish, don't just throw it away—you can throw it across the room if you need to—but hold on to it. You may well find that as you are studying on your own, there'll come a time when you're ready to look back at this book and re-read what I've written. It may be that by then, this book will be helpful in that area, where it wasn't in the beginning.

Most of all, my prayer is that you'll see this book as a tool—as something that can help you. If it doesn't help you, then set it aside for a bit; it might help later.

This book does build on itself, meaning that if you read it in order, you'll get the most out of it. If for some reason you have a specific and urgent question that's answered later on in the book, then feel free to skip ahead. Each chapter does stand at least somewhat alone, and each section can also stand alone.

Lastly, know that the search for truth isn't easy. However, it is so very worth it. In fact, one small detail that God has shown me in my years out of Mormonism is that God is truth. Because He is truth, He values truth and wants us to know truth. What's even better is that He has promised to lead us into all truth!

Most of all, know that it was Jesus Himself who said that we could know the truth, and that truth would set us free. Know that I am praying for you, and most specifically that you would come to know the truth that's in Jesus Christ, and the freedom that's yours in knowing Him, and walking in a relationship with Him.

In Christ,
Katrina Marti

"Thy Word is a lamp unto my feet,
and a light unto my path."

— Psalms 119:105 —

IS THERE TRUTH?

Early in my journey out of the LDS Church, I was praying really, really hard one morning. "Heavenly Father," I said. "The LDS Church is so wonderful: they're strong on family values; they stand for good morals; they have wonderful programs for my kids, and teach me valuable skills that help me as a mother, wife, employee, neighbor. . . ."

Then something really interesting happened to me—Heavenly Father spoke to me. Of course, He didn't speak in an audible voice, nothing that dramatic. Instead, in the way that only He can speak, He said to my heart very clearly: "If only it were true."

That simple statement stopped me in my tracks. How simple, and yet also how true—something can't truly be good by any definition really, if what's at the core of it is a lie.

Not long ago, the news media concentrated heavily on the story of the governor of South Carolina who told the world that he was going on a five-day hiking trip and then simply disappeared.

After he resurfaced, and was hounded by the media for a few weeks, he confessed that he hadn't really been hiking. Instead, he had run off for five days with a woman who was not his wife. As you might have guessed, his wife and sons were deeply hurt, and his chances to run for president in the future (pretty good before) are pretty slim now. I'll reiterate what I said earlier: nothing good can come from a lie.

The trouble is, as the story of the governor illustrates, sometimes it's not so easy to determine truth. Sometimes something can look so very good that we want it to be true, or don't really want to see that it's not true. On the surface it seems good, but we really can't see the lies that are buried deep down inside. I bet you can think of a few local figures in your town who have had that kind of story as well. In Arizona, where I'm from, we had a man who deceived all kinds of folks into putting their retirement funds into his savings and loan company, which was built on lies. His trial was in the news day after day because thousands trusted him and lost everything they owned. They now face the very real possibility of poverty in their retirement days because they believed what was, in essence, a lie.

As members of the LDS Church, we were taught to determine truth based on Moroni 10:4, which tells us, in short, that if we really want to know whether anything is true, we need simply to ask God if it is. If we're earnest, and if we're open-minded, the Holy Ghost will manifest to us whether it's true or not. Maybe that very test is why you joined the church, or, like me, stayed LDS for so long.

The trouble with this test is that it's not really biblical. Instead, the Bible teaches us that our emotions can't be trusted. In the book of Jeremiah, the prophet Jeremiah was continually speaking against false prophets who would prophesy that Israel would be successful in their battles rather than what God had said, which was that they would go into captivity. In the midst of rebuking those prophets God, through Jeremiah, makes a remarkable statement: "The heart is deceitful above all things, and desperately wicked: who can know it?" (Jeremiah 17:9)

In the Bible when the heart is mentioned, it was understood to mean the seat of our will, intellect, and emotions. So, in this verse, God is telling us that He knows that our hearts or our feelings are not to be trusted. Solomon, one of the ancient kings of Israel, who God said was the wisest man of all time, taught: "There is a way which seemeth right unto a man, but the end thereof are the ways of death." (Proverbs 14:12) Literally, what Solomon is telling us is that what we think is "right" often isn't right and can get us in some very real trouble—even death.

In Utah, and perhaps in other places too, swindlers have deceived LDS members by using the Mormon 10:4 test, convincing people to buy into mines, stocks and bonds, banks, and other scams. Maybe you've heard stories like these of people who've prayed, felt that God was directing, and then lost everything that they had invested, sometimes everything they owned. Maybe you've experienced this in your own life where you really, really wanted something, and you've even spent some time praying about it. Maybe you even came to a place that you felt okay about doing it, only to have it hit you in the face that it was a wrong decision. I know I sure have. I witnessed firsthand that my emotions, even those feelings I took to be the Holy Ghost talking to me, could be wrong.

There's a real good reason for this that I'll cover more in the chapter called "Who Am I?" In the meantime, realize that God knew this. He created us and knows way better than we ourselves that our feelings are highly subjective and unreliable. Because He knew us so very well, He didn't leave us to try to figure out what is right and wrong just by thinking about it, praying about it, and feeling something about it. Instead, He gave us His Word, the Bible, which He protected and kept for us to use throughout all time so that we could clearly know who He is, who we are, and how He wants us to approach Him.

An interesting point to note is that Jesus Himself used God's Word in the same way. To see what I mean read Matthew 4, when Satan was tempting Jesus, and note how Jesus responds. In fact, all throughout the New Testament, we find Jesus quoting from scripture and pointing the people around Him back to the Old Testament.[1]

We see in the rest of the New Testament that the apostles continued to use God's Word from which to teach and learn doctrine. There are lots of verses that refer to this, or quote Old Testament scriptures, or teach that we should hold on to the letters that Paul had sent (now the books of Romans through Philemon) or that we should respect what Peter and Paul have taught (that includes the books written by Peter). In short, the Bible itself tells us again and again and again to use it for finding out about God.

A key verse for helping us understand how God wants us to think about the Bible is found in 2 Timothy 3:16-17. It's interesting to note that this verse is written in the context of a time when individual men would apostatize from the truth. In fact, this occurred when men would no longer be interested in what was true, but instead would find teachers who would teach them desirable things. In general, they were looking for things they liked to hear, and wanted to hear. Then, in verse 15, Paul tells Timothy that he, personally, could avoid these pitfalls if he stuck to what he'd been taught directly by Paul and what was in the Old Testament. I suggest you read the whole chapter of this book, but the verse I want to point out is an important one in knowing the way God designed for us to be able to find out truth. It says:

> All scripture is given by inspiration of God, and is profitable for doctrine, for reproof, for correction, for instruction in righteousness: That the man of God may be perfect, thoroughly furnished unto all good works.

Interestingly, in the original language, "all scripture is given by inspiration of God" actually says that scripture is "God-breathed" and that helps us see how God gave us His Word. He inspired, or breathed out, His Word to prophets who wrote it down so that we could know the things He wants us to know.

Look at the list that comes after. It tells us that scripture is profitable, or good for us, in these areas:

- Doctrine,
- Reproof,
- Correction,
- Instruction in righteousness.

It also tells us that with God's Word the man of God can be perfect. The word perfect in the original language means *complete,* meaning that we don't need anything else to do good works, and that we are completely equipped to do good works. Interesting, isn't it?

Let me take a moment and recap that: God breathed into, or inspired, men of old such as prophets, scribes, apostles, and kings to write down what He said to them. With that, He inspired the Word. We, as His followers, can form doctrine, can be corrected when we're wrong, can be admonished when we need it, can learn about righteousness, and are completely and fully equipped to do the good works that God has designed for us. So, in answer to my original question, is there truth? The answer is a resounding yes! There is truth, and that truth can be found in God's inspired Word—the Bible.

Psalms 119 is 176 verses long, and practically the entire Psalm tells us about God's Word, and how a person of God should use it.

Here are a few examples:

[89]Forever, O LORD, thy word is settled in heaven.

[105]Thy word is a lamp unto my feet, and a light unto my path.

[130]The entrance of thy words giveth light; it giveth understanding unto the simple.

[140]Thy word is very pure: therefore thy servant loveth it.

[147-148]I prevented the dawning of the morning, and cried: I hoped in thy word. Mine eyes prevent the night watches, that I might meditate in thy word.

[160]Thy word is true from the beginning: and every one of thy righteous judgments endureth for ever.

There's more in that Psalm as well. Like the rest of the passages I mention here, I highly suggest you read through them.

I started telling you about my conversation with God when He told me that the church was only good if it was actually true, and I'd like to finish by sharing with you a few things I've learned about the truth found in God's Word as I've studied it.

One thing I've learned about God's Word is that God's Word is sometimes painful. It cuts away untruths in our lives and makes us so that we can no longer live with untruth and deception. And personally, too, God's Word plumbs the depth of our hearts to show us what we're really like. It goes deep down inside, to that part we hide from everyone, sometimes even from ourselves. Honestly, you might not like it. I often don't. Hebrews 4:12 warns us of this facet of God's Word:

> For the word of God is quick, and powerful, and sharper than any twoedged sword, piercing even to the dividing asunder of soul and spirit, and of the joints and marrow, and *is* a discerner of the thoughts and intents of the heart.

Another thing I've learned about God's Word is that He's given us everything we need to live a life of godliness. Because it was so important to us, God protected His Word so that even today we can find in it everything we need to know to live this life. 2 Peter 1:3 is where I found this nugget:

> According as his divine power hath given unto us *all things* that pertain unto life and godliness through the knowledge of him that hath called us to glory and virtue: (emphasis mine)

When I first came across this little truth, it was one of those wow moments for me. One of those times when I was just blown away by what God was saying. He hasn't left me lacking and wanting for "more" revelation, "more" guidance, "more" scripture. Instead, He did give me everything I need for life and for godliness; or in other words, for living a godly life. If He's truly given me everything, what more do I really need? In John 8:32, Jesus promised His disciples an amazing thing. He promised them this: "And ye shall know the truth, and the truth shall make you free."

That is just what knowing, and standing on God's eternal truth, does for us. It sets us free! Later on in the same chapter, in verse 36, Jesus reassured His disciples about His truth: "If the Son therefore shall make you free, ye shall be free indeed." And, that's the truth that those of us who have left the LDS Church and entered into biblical Christianity stand on.

Really and truly we are no longer in bondage to try to make something fit into what the Bible teaches. No longer do we have to struggle with our feelings about whether it's true or not, or to pray, pray, pray, until we "know" it's true, only to be blind-sided by another attack and start the cycle of praying, praying, praying, all over again. Instead, we stand, and rest, on the solid ground of what Jesus taught: the truth that sets us free, and that makes us free indeed. You, too, can have that freedom by standing on the solid rock of what God's Word teaches.

---

[1]Whenever Jesus uses the term "the law" or "the prophets," He was referring to the books that now make up our Old Testament. "The Law" are the first five books of the Old Testament, and "the Prophets" are Isaiah through Malachi, and also the historical books of Joshua through Esther. See Matthew 5:17, 7:12, 11:13, 12:5, 22:36-40, Luke 6:4, 10:26, 16:16, 22:44, John 8:17, 10:34, 15:25 for some examples of Jesus talking about the written Word of God.

Chapter Two

CAN I TRUST IT?

One time, while still LDS, I remember studying John 1:1, which says: "In the beginning was the Word, and the Word was with God, and the Word was God."

I remember as an LDS person thinking how this passage seemed to contradict what I'd been taught. It seemed to be saying that Jesus is God the Father, but it surely couldn't have meant that. After reflecting for a bit, I put it aside and ignored it, as I had done with so many other things back then, assuming that somehow the Bible had been translated incorrectly, or that I wasn't understanding it as I should.

That's exactly how we're taught to think when we're LDS. We know, or at least we're taught, that the Bible has been mistranslated and therefore has errors in it. We're not taught what those errors are; so anytime we read something that doesn't seem to agree with our way of thinking, we skip it, thinking "it must be mistranslated." So, has it really been mistranslated like we've been taught?

To answer that question, it's important to understand some concepts about how we got our modern-day Bible. "Transmission" is the first of these. When referring to the Bible, transmission simply means the process of passing the biblical text down from generation to generation. "Translation," on the other hand, is taking a text in one language and putting it into a second. I want to talk about translation more in another chapter, "Which Version Can I Trust?" For now, know that translation means the process of translating the language of the original text into a second language. In our case, that meant taking the text from Greek, Hebrew, and Aramaic and translating it into English.

When LDS Church leaders assure us that the Bible is mistranslated, they are most often actually talking about the process of transmission. Remember that transmission is the process of church leaders and scribes throughout the centuries handing the scrolls, books, and parchments down to the next generation until we have the texts today, which we then translate into English.

Let me illustrate this a bit better. When I was LDS, I understood the passing on, or transmission, of the Bible in this way: There was a church leader who led for, say, fifty years. He notices that the parchments are getting old, so he has his scribe copy over a new one. In the process, this scribe makes a mistake on a few words, and no one catches his mistake. This new text then becomes the Authorized Version, complete with its mistakes. The next generation comes along, let's say fifty years later, and this time the church leader is kind of a messed-up guy. He, too, has his scribe make a copy of the Bible, and it was from the corrected, or messed-up, text. This time, the leader has him change some passages he doesn't like. For instance, maybe he inserts a command for money to be given to him. Then the next generation comes along. This time, the leader is a good guy, so he just has the new text made from the old one. However, he also notices that some passages no longer make sense because of the first scribe's mistake, or because of the crooked guy's additions. He now adds words to make them make sense, or just leaves out passages altogether so that once again it makes sense. So, the cycle goes on. Each generation adds, takes away, fixes up, or just plain changes the text until we get our current Bible. It's still a pretty good document, but kind of messed up by men throughout the generations, and certainly not very trustworthy.

The truth, though, is that this is not at all what happened—at least not in the big picture of the transmission of the Bible. Instead, each generation of translators, or scribes, went as far back as they could go. They searched diligently among all the ancient texts, and there are thousands. Some that exist today date as far back as the third century. From all of these—the whole of it, and not just any one document—they would make the most accurate translation possible for each generation, including our own. The interesting thing is that quite recently ancient scripture like the Dead Sea Scrolls, which were written before, and just after Jesus lived, have been discovered. And they agree—practically without any difference—with the Bible we have today. Why? Because of the care that men of God have taken throughout the generations in remaining true to the original text.

To illustrate this process, let's try to chart it out as shown on the next page.

What the LDS Church Taught Us Happened

Original Text: Paul, an apostle of Jesus Christ by the will of God, to the saints which are at Ephesus, and to the faithful in Christ Jesus:… (Ephesians 1:1)

Scribe one copy around A.D. 100: Paul, an apostle of Jesus Christ by the will of the brethren, to the saints which are at Ephesus and to the faithful in Christ Jesus:…

Scribe two copy around A.D. 150: Paul, an apostle of Jesus Christ by vote of the brethren, to the saints which are at Ephesus and to the faithful in Christ Jesus:…

Scribe three copy around A.D. 200: Paul, an apostle of Jesus Christ by vote of the church, to the saints which are at Ephesus and to the faithful in Christ Jesus:…

Scribe four copy around A.D. 250: Paul, an apostle of Jesus Christ by vote of the other elders, to the saints which are at Ephesus and to the faithful in Christ Jesus:…

On and on, until today, it might say:

Paul, a good person who loves Jesus Christ by vote of the church, to the faithful, which are at any church, and to the good ones who are on this same boat with me:

What Really Happened

Text one was written by Paul directly:

Paul, an apostle of Jesus Christ by the will of God, to the saints which are at Ephesus, and to the faithful in Christ Jesus:… (Ephesians 1:1)

The churches made copies of Paul's letter and distributed them to all the churches.

> Paul, an apostle of Jesus Christ by the will of God, to the saints which are at Ephesus, and to the faithful in Christ Jesus:… (Ephesians 1:1)

When it was time for the canon of scripture to be put together, the scholars went back to all those letters and made the most accurate copy possible.

> Paul, an apostle of Jesus Christ by the will of God, to the saints which are at Ephesus, and to the faithful in Christ Jesus:… (Ephesians 1:1)

As time went on, when a new copy was made, scholars went to those oldest texts and pulled together, as accurately as possible, a clean text. They used the original documents, where available, and the oldest possible texts, where it wasn't available.

> Paul, an apostle of Jesus Christ by the will of God, to the saints which are at Ephesus, and to the faithful in Christ Jesus:… (Ephesians 1:1)

In 1611, scholars who worked for King James pulled all those oldest manuscripts together and from all of those manuscripts written in Latin, Greek, and Aramaic translated the Bible into English. That was the "original" King James Version (KJV).

> Paul, an apostle of Jesus Christ by the will of God, to the saints which are at Ephesus, and to the faithful in Christ Jesus:… (Ephesians 1:1)

In the last two hundred years, in addition to the Dead Sea Scrolls, many very old manuscripts have been found. They were compared with what was the prior oldest manuscript, checked for accuracy, and then compiled into a manuscript that translators could then translate into English.

> Paul, an apostle of Jesus Christ by the will of God, to the saints which are at Ephesus, and to the faithful in Christ Jesus:... (Ephesians 1:1)

To explain more about the care taken with the manuscripts, let's first go to the Old Testament. That's perhaps the most interesting because Hebrew scribes had great respect for not just every single letter in the Bible but for every single jot and tittle (equivalent to our crossing our t's and dotting our i's). So, when Hebrew scribes copied a scroll, they went to great lengths to make sure that every single little tiny mark was copied as well. They even went to the point of counting how many letters were in a line, making sure the new line had the same number of letters, and then counting to the middle and making sure the middle of the new line lined up.

The Talmud, or the Jewish handbook for life, gave scribes painstaking rules they had to follow when copying the biblical texts. Here are a few of those rules:

- They could only use clean animal skins, both to write on, and even to bind manuscripts.
- Each column of writing could have no less than forty-eight lines, and no more than sixty.
- The ink must be black, and of a special recipe.
- They must verbalize each word aloud while they were writing.
- Every time before writing the word "Jehovah," they must wipe the pen and wash their entire bodies.
- The letters, words, and paragraphs had to be counted, and the document became invalid if two letters touched each other. The middle paragraph, words and letters, must correspond to those of the original document.

- They couldn't write anything from memory but instead must look at the script from which they were copying.

The New Testament was treated just as carefully, the difference being that originally the New Testament was written as a series of letters—letters that were meant to be copied and shared with each and every church. There was generally a church, or two, in every town that met in someone's house, and the churches had their appointed leaders who led the group and helped them stay true to sound doctrine. (We'll talk more about this in the chapter about choosing a church.) So, over time there became a proliferation of these letters floating around. Eventually someone put these letters together and created the book that we call the New Testament. The end result, though, is that there are hundreds of old manuscripts that together show us the accuracy of what we call our Bible today.

There's a whole science that goes into figuring out which of the ancient texts to put together to form the most accurate manuscript possible. It gets very technical. We won't go into that here. Suffice it to say, we can trust that the manuscript we have today is more accurate than any other type of ancient manuscript anywhere. It has been tested over and over again and has been found to be accurate in every detail. (One way was by comparing them with some of the newly discovered ancient manuscripts, as I mentioned before.)

Another important test of New Testament accuracy is found in the writings of the earliest church fathers, some of whom were contemporaries of John. They, too, used as their source the New Testament manuscripts, in some cases, originals, which are now lost to time. They would often quote from these sources throughout their teaching lesson (similar to what I'm doing in this book). What's exciting about all of this is, if for some reason we didn't have the manuscripts that we have now, we could actually go back to these lessons and recreate the entire New Testament from the quotes in these lessons. These writings agree completely with the manuscript we have today.

A third test of the Bible's accuracy comes in the bulk of physical evidence that backs it up. You probably know that you can go to Israel today and see many of the sights that are mentioned from Jesus' day in the Bible. Not only can you visit New Testament sites, but you can visit many of the very ancient sites of the Old Testament as well. Did you know that archaeologists have found the site of the ancient city of Jericho? And they discovered something very interesting that verifies one of the details from the Bible: they found that the walls of Jericho fell outward, not inward as they normally would have if the battle had been fought in the normal way of an army outside breaking down the defensive walls of the city. Joshua 6 tells the story of the conquest of Jericho. It's a fascinating story and shares the detail that when the people blew their trumpets and shouted, the walls of the city fell down rather than being battered and falling inwardly as they would normally when a city wall was breached in battle. This is just one small story in the Bible whose details have been confirmed by modern-day archeology. There are literally hundreds of these details, right down to the finding of the names of insignificant kings and their servants, and these have been confirmed by scientists today. Conversely, no significant find by archaeologists has ever refuted a biblical reference.

Lastly, know that the final and perhaps most convincing "proof" of the fact that we can trust the Bible is that God Himself tells us to trust it. Last chapter I mentioned my discovery of 2 Peter 1:3

that says: "According as his divine power hath given unto us all things that pertain unto life and godliness,…"

Throughout the Bible, we see God telling us to trust His Word, and that His Word is sufficient for living the Christian life. Here are some examples:

> Knowing this first, that no prophecy of the scripture is of any private interpretation. For the prophecy came not in old time by the will of man: but holy men of God spake as they were moved by the Holy Ghost. (2 Peter 1:20-21)

> Now we beseech you, brethren,…That ye be not soon shaken in mind, or be troubled, neither by spirit, nor by word, nor by letter as from us, as that the day of Christ is at hand. Let no man deceive you by any means. Therefore, brethren, stand fast, and hold the traditions which ye have been taught, whether by word, or our epistle. (2 Thessalonians 2:1-15 abbreviated)

> This know also, that in the last days perilous times shall come… But continue thou in the things which thou hast learned and hast been assured of, knowing of whom thou hast learned them; And that from a child thou hast known the holy scriptures, which are able to make thee wise unto salvation through faith which is in Christ Jesus.
> (2 Timothy 3:1-15 abbreviated)

> He said unto him, "What is written in the law? how readest thou?" (Luke 10:26, Jesus talking to the lawyer)

> And he said unto them, "Have ye never read what David did, when he had need, and was hungered, he,

and they that were with him?" (Mark 2:25, Jesus talking to the Pharisees talking about what we read in 1 Samuel 21:1)

And said unto him, "Hearest thou what these say?" And Jesus saith unto them, "Yea; have ye never read, Out of the mouth of babes and sucklings thou hast perfected praise?" (Matthew 21:16, Jesus responding to the leaders and chief scribes and quoting Psalms 8:2)

"And I say also unto thee, That thou art Peter, and upon this rock I will build my church; and the gates of hell shall not prevail against it." (Matthew 16:18)

Another strong reason for trusting the Bible we have today points to God Himself. If the God of the Universe, who created all things, who upholds the world by the power of His will, who created you and me and all things in the world, says that we should trust His Word, what more do we really need? If God could do all those things that I mentioned above, surely He could keep His Word, and preserve His Word just as He says He would. What's more, He knew that there'd be lots of deception out there, and He knew that you and I would be skeptical. For that reason, He even provided evidence that points to Him having protected His Word, just as He said He would. In fact, He's provided more evidence than would be needed in any court trial, in any scientific proof, or medical trial. We trust their results. In fact, we stake our lives on their results. Isn't it interesting that we want God to give us more? Do we really need more?

Chapter Three

WHICH VERSION CAN I TRUST?

Friend,

Every time I think of you, I give thanks to my God. I pray that your love will overflow more and more, and that you will keep on growing in knowledge and understanding. For I want you to understand what really matters, so that you may live pure and blameless lives until the day of Christ's return.[1] We also pray that you will be strengthened with all his glorious power so you will have all the endurance and patience you need.[2] May you be filled with joy, always thanking the Father.[3] When I think of all this, I fall to my knees and pray to the Father, the Creator of everything in heaven and on earth.[4] I pray that from his glorious, unlimited resources he will empower you with inner strength through his Spirit. Then Christ will make his home in your hearts as you trust in him. Your roots will grow down into God's love and keep you strong. And may you have the power to understand, as all God's people should, how wide, how long, how high, and how deep his love is. May you experience the love of Christ, though it is too great to understand fully. Then you will be made complete with all the fullness of life and power that comes from God.[5]

When I first read these passages from the New Living Translation of the Bible (taken from the books of Ephesians, Galatians, and Philippians), I was blown away. It seemed to me that Paul, inspired by the Holy Spirit, was speaking these words directly to me. It was like a love letter sent to me from God. It really was an amazing experience. That is why I wanted to write this chapter about which version, or translation, of the Bible you should read. It has to do with God's design in writing the Bible. His plan is to give you a reference book, if you will, that you can understand completely, and in that understanding, see His great love for you.

When Peter, Paul, John, and the rest were writing their letters, they wrote them specifically to individual churches, or groups of individuals, with the intent that they be copied and passed around to all the churches so that everyone could read them. For that purpose, the letters were written simply and in the language of the common people of that day. Today, just as in that day, God wants us to understand His Word. Therefore, the intent of any good Bible translation should be to be understood.

I want to state here unequivocally that you can continue to read the KJV if you want. It's a very accurate translation of the Bible. I would, however, suggest that you get a non-LDS version so you don't have to deal with chapter heads and footnotes that point you to LDS resources or refer you to LDS doctrine. As you study more and more, I think you'll find the LDS stuff confusing.

That is something you definitely don't need at this stage in the journey. You actually can buy KJV Bibles with no extraneous footnotes, chapter heads, or anything extra at all. At this point, that might be a good idea.

Before I go any further, though, let me explain a bit about the translation process. Remember in the last chapter we talked about transmission, or the passing of the manuscripts down through the generations.

First know that just about every group that translates the Bible into our modern language desires to convey the Word of God in as accurate and understandable a manner as possible. They want you to know what God has said, and they want you to understand that as quickly, easily, and clearly as possible. William Tyndale, the very first translator of the English Bible, was actually killed because of his desire to make the Bible understandable to the common person.

Within that desire to make the Bible understandable to everyone, there are basically two ways that a text can be translated: The first method is to translate the Bible word for word. On the surface, that sounds like a very reasonable way to do it. The trouble, however, is that it's not quite that easy. I'm no translator (nor do I want to be—that's a hard job!), but I do speak Spanish.

A rather easy illustration from Spanish may show you what I'm talking about: El leon no es como lo pintan. Translating this statement, word for word, it would say: "The lion no is how it they paint."

In English, word-for-word translation of this particular statement just doesn't work. It really doesn't make much sense to us. That's true of many statements in the Bible. To make sense of these, translators have had to change word order, sometimes change the whole statement, and sometimes even have to use a different word altogether, one that is more appropriate for the target language. So, a translator who was translating my Spanish statement into English in a word-for-word translation would probably translate it as "The lion isn't how they paint it."

It's a great translation, as far as being accurate. However, if you're not familiar with this particular saying in Spanish, you might have a hard time understanding it if the translator stopped here in his translation. Translations of the Bible, such as the King James Version (KJV), New American Standard Bible (NASB), Revised Standard Version (RSV), and New King James Version (NKJV), all are done using a more or less word-for-word translation, but changing things only where they don't make sense. This is why you'll see the italicized words in the KJV; they're additions to the text without which it just wouldn't mean the same thing in English.

The drawback to word-for-word translations is that they sometimes read a bit choppy, are usually less poetic, and can be a bit harder to understand. Also, translations using this method usually read at a higher-grade level than ones translated using the other method. The King James Version, for example, is written at about a twelfth-grade level, making it extremely difficult for children or the less educated to understand clearly.

The second method used in translating the Bible is a thought-for-thought translation. Some of the versions that use this method of translation are the New International Version (NIV), New Living Translation (NLT), and Contemporary English Version (CEV). Translators working on these translations went to the original language and worked real hard to figure out what the writer meant to convey. Then they conveyed that in the target language, often changing some of the words, or the word order to do this. My example of El leon no es como lo pintan might be translated in a thought-for-thought manner as "You've got to look deeper than face value on this issue because what we see up front is not necessarily what the truth is."

The nice thing about a thought-for-thought translation is that it reads much more like how we talk. That is because it is actual speech as we use it today, or at least when it was published.

Another aspect of this type of translation is that the translators often go to great lengths to make every single word they use understandable to the general public. We can see this by studying this passage from Romans 3:25 from the King James Version, which says:

> Whom God hath set forth to be a propitiation through faith in his blood, to declare his righteousness for the remission of sins that are past, through the forbearance of God;

We can contrast and compare that version to the New Living Translation:

> For God presented Jesus as the sacrifice for sin. People are made right with God when they believe that Jesus sacrificed his life, shedding his blood. This sacrifice shows that God was being fair when he held back and did not punish those who sinned in times past,

As you can see, the NLT is a bit longer but it portrays the same thoughts as the KJV. However, words like remission of sin, propitiation, righteousness, and forbearance are explained for the benefit of those who might not understand them.

Another major benefit of most of the thought-for-thought translations is that they're written at lower-grade levels than the word-for-word translations, making it easier for you and me to understand, and also making them a good choice for our children who aren't yet twelfth-grade readers.

Now that we understand the method of translation, let's talk about the final issue involved in Bible translation: what manuscripts are used in the translation. I mentioned in the last chapter the hundreds of manuscripts that today's modern translators have available to them; not to mention that all of the New Testament originally was composed of separate letters. Imagine trying to work surrounded by all those manuscripts! This is wonderful when looking for accuracy, but you can imagine the translator's frustration if they tried to work with all these manuscripts (not to mention they're spread out all over the world).

Instead of attempting that monumental feat, those who are in that field have coalesced two main manuscripts that they then use for translation: the first is called the Textus Receptus and was compiled before the year 1610 when the King James Version was put together. The second manuscript is a newer version of the same thing. It is called the Westcott and Hort text, which is named after the scholars who put it together, and uses manuscripts discovered after that time, as well as the manuscripts that the Textus Receptus people used. There's a huge controversy over these texts, and I won't go into it here. If you want, you can read more about that controversy; and at some point in your Christian life, you'll probably want to do that. For now, know that the KJV and NKJV use the Textus Receptus as their base text, and the NASB, NIV, and most of the other newer translations use the Westcott and Hort text.

So, back to the original question: which translation should I use? The bottom line is that you can use with confidence any of the ones I've mentioned in this chapter. They're all great translations and they've all got something to offer. I would highly suggest using a version, at least initially, that's different from the KJV. The reason I suggest that is that you'll find your eyes opening up a lot when you read something familiar but said in a different way. The same thing has happened to me this past year as I've started reading from a Spanish Bible. I find myself seeing things I've never seen before, simply because it's a new way of saying the same old thing.

Another thing I'd highly suggest is to read through the New Testament at least once in one of the newer, thought-for-thought translations. I think you'll find it an eye-opening experience. The first time I picked up the New Living Translation, I was amazed by Paul's letters. Suddenly they came alive and I could see them for the first time as a letter written to me by a friend, which was Paul's intent. It was an amazing experience, and one I'd highly recommend for you.

Most Christians, including me, use a variety of Bible translations for studying. It's a good idea. Sometimes one translation will say it in a more understandable way, or will use a word that speaks to me personally. Most serious scholars, in general, use a word-for-word translation for serious study, as well as other study resources, which I'll talk about in a minute. Another option for study purposes would be the Amplified Version. The translators of the New American Standard Version translated this one too. However, instead of choosing one word to translate for one word, they chose to use every possible adjective it could be, so you can see every possible meaning of that word or passage. I find it too tedious to read all the time. Once in a while, though, it's a very interesting experience to refer to it.

For serious study, you might also want to check out Strong's Concordance and Vine's Expository Dictionary of New Testament Words. With these two tools, you can actually look up the word you're studying in the original language and see for yourself every possible meaning of that word. An online resource that has these included is the Blue Letter Bible at www.blueletterbible.org. It's much less tedious to use than the book versions of these two. Biblegateway.org is another of my favorite tools to use online. With it, you can search for any word in the Bible and read it in all the major translations, and in some of the minor ones too. In fact, this is a great resource to "check out" translations. It enables you to read the same passage in a number of ways before you settle on, and then spend money on, a new Bible.

Another thing that can be very helpful is a good study Bible. In a study Bible, the editor puts in side notes, helpful small articles explaining the text, and cross-references that help you understand what the text is saying or points out things you should be thinking about. You can find study Bibles for new believers, as well as for just about any special area, such as women, men, children, teens, alcoholics, or people with addictions, to name some.

I don't know what issues in the church have led you away. For me, it was really seeing where doctrines in the Bible just didn't jibe with doctrines I'd been taught my whole life. It's interesting to realize that at the time I really didn't trust the text of the Bible. However, after much study, I've come to see that the text of the Bible is accurate and can be trusted. God designed the Bible to be understandable to me. For me, that meant getting away from the King James Version of the Bible. Honestly, to this day, I don't like to read from it. For you, it may include using the King James Version. It's really up to you. What's important to know is that God has given us His Word today in order to be able to find truth. His Word can help us to form doctrine, to correct us,

to teach us what we need to know to serve Him. In that process, He's maintained His Word for us, and it's just as relevant to us today as it has been throughout the ages.

---

[1]Philippians 1:3; 9-10 New Living Translation. [2]Colossians 1:11 New Living Translation. [3]Colossians 1:11b, 12a New Living Translation. [4]Ephesians 3:14-15 New Living Translation. [5]Ephesians 3:16-19 New Living Translation.

"But these are written,
that ye might believe that Jesus is the Christ,
the Son of God;
and that believing ye might have life
through his name."

— John 20:31 —

Chapter Four

WHAT SHOULD I READ?

The Bible is a huge book—66 books, 1,189 chapters, and 31,173 verses, and it can be overwhelming to start reading it. So, I'd like to suggest a few things:

First, do it in small chunks. Remember God sent His Word to teach us doctrine, to correct us, to discipline us, to teach us about Him, and to perfect us. He intended to help us see things from His point of view rather than our own. Sometimes you'll find a passage is very deep, and one verse may be enough to think about for a time; other times you'll skip through a passage more quickly.

Also know that the Bible was not originally written in chapters and verses; those were later additions. As such, those additions are not inspired, although helpful. Sometimes you'll find it a lot more beneficial (and a lot more understandable) to read from paragraph to paragraph rather than chapter to chapter. The reason is that paragraphs usually include a complete thought.

Another thing I'd highly suggest is to start your reading in the book of John. John says that his purpose in writing this book is, "that ye might believe that Jesus is the Christ." That's why it's a great place to start:

> But these are written, that ye might believe that Jesus is the Christ, the Son of God; and that believing ye might have life through his name. (John 20:31)

From the book of John, I'd suggest you read Mark, then Acts, Romans, and Galatians. That'll give you a real good overview of what the New Testament is all about. From there, I'd highly suggest you read the book of Genesis. Things that happen in Genesis set the stage for everything else that happens in the Bible, so it's important to understand what it teaches.

From there, you can go pretty much anywhere you want. Some people I know make a point of reading at least one Psalm daily. Because the book of Proverbs is about wisdom, and because there are 31 chapters, many people find it handy to read one of them every day of the month. Other people want to read the Bible chronologically, or as it was written. There are charts you can get online to help you to do this. It's a very interesting way to read the Bible.

In the end, it doesn't really matter in what order you read, but it's a good thing to put together a plan to read the Bible in about a year. You have to read about three chapters a day to accomplish that. For me, I've taken to reading one chapter in at least six different sections of the Bible, which correspond with every major break in the Bible. The five books of Moses are one section; the historical books of Joshua through Job are another; the poetic books are another; the prophets (Isaiah through Malachi) are another; the gospels and Acts another, and the epistles with Revelation another. For me, this helps to break up things. Honestly, if I'm in a hard place to read—one with lots of genealogies, for instance—it helps me stick with it if I break it up into smaller chunks.

Another thing that can be a real good tool is to keep a small notebook handy as you read. You can note verses that God uses to send you a special message—like a reminder not to gossip or to always tell the truth. You can keep track of things you want to study—like the nature of God, or the nature of man, or really just about any issue you want to pursue. This is a tool I used when I was trying to understand who God was, especially looking at the Christian doctrine of the trinity. I spent about nine months reading and very thoroughly noting every single instance where the character of God was mentioned. Then after those months of noting them, I was able to put them all together and see for myself what the Bible taught about God.

Something else that is a real good idea, although intimidating, is to take small portions of scripture and work on committing them to memory. Now before you scream at me, "I can't memorize anything!" rest assured I can't either. However, as I've taken a small portion of scripture and spent fifteen minutes a day memorizing it, an amazing thing has happened: I've seen things in that passage that I never, ever saw before. Two weeks later, I can't quote you that verse, but you know what? I can tell you where it is in the Bible, and I can tell you the "Katrina's paraphrased version." What happens when we memorize is that we meditate on the verse, and scripturally speaking we hide God's truth in our hearts, where He can later retrieve it just when we need it most. Trust me when I say there's no pressure here; I resisted memorizing scripture for several years—truly. After having done it, though, I would have to tell you it's one of the most valuable things I've ever done.

In the end, I have to repeat Nike's advertising slogan "Just Do It." When it comes to Bible reading, it's the most important thing to remember. In fact, it doesn't really matter how you do it at all. It just matters that you do!

Chapter Five

WHICH CHURCH
IS THE TRUE CHURCH?

ur first Sunday out of the LDS Church, we visited, purely by chance, a little Southern Baptist Church in my hometown. It wasn't my first choice—believe me. I was scared to death of *those* Southern Baptists. We chose it for the very logical reason that it had the latest worship service in town, and our infant daughter had been up until the wee hours.

Lucky for us, God used all those circumstances to bring us to a church that was perfect for what we needed at that time. My point in sharing this with you is to encourage you that at least in the beginning, your fumbling around and looking for a new church doesn't have to be perfect. God can and will use the circumstances of your life to put you right where He wants you.

I also want to say that I don't think at all that the Southern Baptist Church is *the* true church. Since going to that church, my husband and I have had the opportunity to visit just about every denomination of church within the traditional Christian banner.

We have enjoyed things about just about every one. The reason for that is because that is the true church.

What do you mean? you say. Well, let me explain biblically what *the* church really is. You see, from a biblical point of view, the true church is made up of all those who have put their faith in Jesus Christ anywhere in the world, and in all kinds of denominations. I'll explain more about what putting your faith in Jesus Christ means in the chapter "What Does God Want from Me?" But for now, stick with me and let me explain about the true church.

Before that, though, I want to share with you one of my favorite passages in the Bible. It starts out with John, who wrote the book of Revelation, looking into a scene in heaven. In that scene, there's a book that no one can open, because everyone, and every creature, was tainted. Just as John starts to weep because of his despair over this turn of events, someone points out to him that there is One who is worthy to open the book: Jesus Christ. Jesus then takes the book to open it. When he does, the creatures that surround Jesus fall down on their faces in utter devotion and start singing, "Thou art worthy to take up the book. . . ." Then the scene opens up, and the Bible says that there were ten thousands times ten thousands, and thousands and thousands (or, in other words, a huge crowd) praising Jesus from every culture, language, people, and time.

This scene really speaks to my heart because it talks about who the church is here today on earth: all of those who have been redeemed of the Lord.

When we were LDS, as you know, the LDS Church was a specific object: an organization that had Jesus' power to represent Him here on earth. For a person to really reach the potential that God intended for him, they had to do certain things within the church or they were lost to a lower king-dom throughout the eternities. The LDS Church also had a special power that was delegated to it by God Himself to do all the things that are required of its members here on earth. (We'll talk more about the issue of the priesthood in the chap-ter called, "By Whose Authority.")

The Bible, however, doesn't talk about an organization as the church. Instead, it talks about "assemblies " or groups of people who have put their faith in Jesus Christ. We see this in passages such as Acts 2:47, where those who were saved were "added" to the church, or in passages such as Acts 5:11, where it talks about "great fear" coming on the church, meaning all those who had believed, and not just one particular organization. We see it also in Ephesians where it talks about the church as the body of Christ, where He, Himself, is the head.

There are instances, though, in the Bible where it does talk about specific groups of people and calls them a church, or as-sembly.[1] In those cases, what usually is talked about is all those who lived in a particular area, such as when it talks about the church in Ephesus, or Philippi. Early church history shows that the New Testament church did indeed usually start out as groups of people who believed in Jesus and then met together in each other's homes. It's important to note, though, that never is a name given for this church, nor a specific hierarchal authority to do things. Instead, these biblical churches are referred to as "the church that meets in so and so's house" or the church of Laodi-cea, or Corinth, or Philippi, all cities in Bible times. In this way again, the Bible is referring to a group of people who lived in a certain area, and not an organization.

In addition to the Bible using the word "church" to describe the body of believers, scripture also talks about the true church by calling it "the body of Christ." We see this several places in the Bible. Ephesians 1:22-23 is probably the best example and says:

> ...And hath put all things under his feet, and gave
> him to be the head over all things to the church,
> Which is his body, the fulness of him that filleth all
> in all.

1 Corinthians 12:13 tells us how we get put into that body and reiterates that we are one body, and not just a bunch of bodies, or even a select body. It says: "For by one Spirit are we all baptized into one body,..."

Ephesians 4 also reiterates that as believers we all belong to one body, and have one faith:

> There is one body, and one Spirit, even as ye are
> called in one hope of your calling; One Lord, one
> faith, one baptism,...

So, when Christians talk about the true church, they're really referring to the body of believers, or all people everywhere, from every time, who have put their faith in Christ. As such, when we talk about the church biblically, we could be referring to a small group meeting together in Ethiopia or a megachurch in Brazil, or a Southern Baptist church in Arizona or a Methodist church in Louisiana, or, well, you get the picture. All of these together make up the church. (Note: not all people who go to an organized church are people who have put their faith in Jesus Christ. So, it's not really accurate for us to say, for instance, that everyone who's a member of that little Southern Baptist church in my hometown really belongs to the church, but rather that they attend a church.)

So, the first principle we've got to understand is that the true church consists of all believers everywhere, and from all times. That, biblically speaking, is the true church.

However, the Bible also teaches that the local church, or the actual place that we go to meet together with those other believers, is important. The book of Hebrews actually teaches us that we shouldn't forsake the gathering of ourselves together. Or, in other words, we should meet together.

The Bible goes into great detail telling us why we should meet together. You see, God designed us to be a body that works together for His glory. Maybe a better way to describe it would be to define it as a living organism that works in tandem. In fact, three different passages in the Bible talk about the idea of us working together for God's glory. Let's look at those just for a moment:

> For as we have many members in one body, and all members have not the same office: So we, being many, are one body in Christ, and every one members one of another. Having then gifts differing according to the grace that is given to us, …(Romans 12:4-6a)
> For as the body is one, and hath many members, and all the members of that one body, being many, are one body: so also is Christ. For by one Spirit are we all baptized into one body, whether we be Jews or Gentiles, whether we be bond or free; and have been all made to drink into one Spirit. For the body is not one member, but many. If the foot shall say, Because I am not the hand, I am not of the body; is it therefore not of the body? And if the ear shall say, Because I am not the eye, I am not of the body;

is it therefore not of the body? If the whole body were an eye, where were the hearing? If the whole were hearing, where were the smelling? But now hath God set the members every one of them in the body, as it hath pleased him. And if they were all one member, where were the body? But now are they many members, yet but one body. And the eye cannot say unto the hand, I have no need of thee: nor again the head to the feet, I have no need of you. Nay, much more those members of the body, which seem to be more feeble, are necessary: And those members of the body, which we think to be less honourable, upon these we bestow more abundant honour; and our uncomely parts have more abundant comeliness. For our comely parts have no need: but God hath tempered the body together, having given more abundant honour to that part which lacked. That there should be no schism in the body; but that the members should have the same care one for another. And whether one member suffer, all the members suffer with it; or one member be honoured, all the members rejoice with it. Now ye are the body of Christ, and members in particular. (1 Corinthians 12:12-27)

And He gave some apostles, some prophets, and some, evangelists; and some, pastors and teachers; for the perfecting of the saints, for the work of the ministry, for the edifying of the body of Christ; till we all come in the unity of the faith and of the knowledge of the Son of God, unto a perfect man, unto the

measure of the stature of the fullness of Christ; that
we henceforth be no more children. . .may grow up
into Him in all things, which is the head, even Christ.
(Ephesians 4:12-15)

You see, God's design for His true church is that we each would
function together, growing and building each other up: encouraging each other, teaching each other, ministering to each other.
In that, we would grow together to know Him more and more,
and give Him glory. The only place we can do that, really, is in
a local church.

I'm going to talk a bit more about that in the chapter entitled
"Why Go To Church," but for now keep in mind that God has a
plan for both the local church and the universal church. While
there are many, many denominations out there, God will put us
exactly where He wants us to be, both for our own growth, and
so that we can serve within the church.

---

[1]The Greek word that's most often translated "church" in the New Testament in its
simplest form means assembly.

"There is one body, and one Spirit,
even as ye are called
in one hope of your calling;"
— Ephesians 4:4 —

Chapter Six

SO, ARE ALL CHURCHES
THE TRUE CHURCH?

While my choice of going to a Southern Baptist church, based on a sleepless night, might not be good criteria for choosing a church, God did lead us to a church that was very serious about taking all of their doctrine from the Bible. That is the first and best criteria we should use for choosing a good church. However, as you may have seen, there are thousands of choices in Christianity. Most, if not all, claiming to be biblically based. So choosing a church, especially to us ex-Mormons, can be a daunting task. In this chapter, I want to explore the issue of denominations, and how we should look at them, biblically, as we're in the process of choosing a church.

There's a saying in the church that is generally attributed to St. Augustine, a Catholic priest and church father who lived from A.D. 354–430. It explains some of the differences between Christian denominations, and it helps us see a godly response to the differences among denominations: "In Essentials, Unity; in Non-essentials, Liberty; in All Things, Charity."

As we noted in the last chapter, "Which Church Is the True Church?" the true church is made up of all people who have put their faith in Jesus in all types of biblically based churches. However, as we already know, most Christians would not accept churches like The Church of Jesus Christ of Latter Day Saints as members of the true church. To understand why that is, we need to look a bit deeper at what the Bible teaches and realize that there are some doctrines, more commonly referred to as "essentials," that are so clearly spelled out that there is virtually no dispute between denominations. There are other doctrines, or "nonessentials," that could be the basis for two or more different and good arguments based on the Bible alone.

An example of that may be found in the practice of celebrating Christmas. I could make an argument, biblically, that because we're celebrating Jesus' birth, a biblical event, we should celebrate Christmas in much the same way the rest of America celebrates. However, another group of Christians could also make an argument *from the Bible* that celebrating Jesus' birth in the way that Americans celebrate is not something Christians should do. This would be an issue that would be considered nonessential. It's not because it's not important. Rather, because while two arguments could be made biblically, we ultimately can't settle this issue by going to the Bible alone. Instead, we have to rely on how God is speaking to each of us individually. The Bible commands us to work through issues like this with God, in fact, and to respond as He directs each of us individually.

Essentials, on the other hand, are those doctrines that the Bible is absolutely clear about, with no real room for differences of opinion. Here's a list of what most Christians, who get their doctrine from the Bible alone, would consider essentials:

- The Deity of Jesus Christ
- Salvation by grace alone, by faith alone
- The physical resurrection of Jesus
- Jesus' virgin birth
- Belief in Jesus as the only way to salvation
- The trinity
- Monotheism (the belief in only one God)
- The authority and inerrancy of scripture
- The nature of God
- The nature of mankind
- The biblical fact that all men sin and are separate from a Holy God by that sin
- The nature of the Holy Spirit.

On the other hand, there are other doctrines in Christianity that when we look at the Bible, we can make a good argument for more than one belief. These would include doctrines like:

- A belief that certain spiritual gifts have ceased today or conversely have not ceased and should be in operation in the church today
- A belief that man is capable of putting his faith in Jesus, or that man is totally unable to do anything at all to contribute to his salvation, and therefore God has to do a work to even allow the man to put his faith in Jesus (these two ways of looking at scripture are generally referred to as Arminianism and Calvinism)
- Differences in how we think end-time events will play out
- Beliefs that center around how a church should be led and/or structured
- When, how, who, and even why we should be baptized
- The style of worship: casual, conservative, and more

- Celebrating certain holidays, or not
- Plus, more!

I won't go into all the details of these issues now. Suffice it to say that in Christianity, these issues are what divide churches, or are why we have so many denominations today.

Initially you honestly won't know where you stand on all these issues. It can take years to figure out where you stand on these issues. Right now, you're grappling with some other much bigger, and much more important, issues. You might have some strong feelings about some of them—right or wrong. For instance, if you feel strongly that speaking in tongues is something that doesn't happen today, you may want to stay away from churches that claim to be Pentecostal, charismatic, spirit-filled, or full-gospel. Keep in mind, though, that this is not one of the essential doctrines of the Christian faith, and that the people in those churches are just as much a part of the church as someone belonging to a more conservative denomination.

So, to recap a bit here, the most important thing to look at when looking at a church is how they treat the Bible. Do they consider it their authority? Or do they accept something else as equally or more true? If they consider the Bible as their ultimate authority for setting doctrine, most likely they'll believe fully in those essential Christian doctrines that I have mentioned above. I'll be talking more about some of those essential doctrines in the next few chapters, and you've got time to study them and see what I mean. For now, you'll just have to trust me and two thousand years of biblical scholarship on this.

It's also interesting to note that in nearly every single instance where a church rejects one or more of these essential doctrines, that church has accepted some form of extra-biblical revelation as their source for truth. Some examples include: the Catholic Church, which accepts the pope and papal decrees as more important than scripture; the LDS Church, whose standard of truth is the modern prophet; and Jehovah's Witnesses, who have their own translation of the Bible that agrees with what their leaders teach. The reason it's interesting is because this is exactly how Satan works. We'll talk a bit more about him and his schemes in the chapter titled, "Who Am I," but for now know that one of the ways Satan works is to add to, or take away from, God's Word. For an example of this, you can read Genesis 3 where Satan tempts Eve and see for yourself how he casts doubt on God's Word.

So, to answer our original question of "Are all churches true?", the response is a resounding no! Rather, churches that use God's standard of truth, the Bible, as their standard of truth are sure to have a good portion of their members belonging to "the true church" or "body of Christ."

Before we go on to other not-so-important things that you'll want to think about when choosing a church, I want to mention the issue of worship music. Chances are, if you've ever attended a Christian church, you've been a bit disturbed by the boisterous worship music, clapping, raising of hands, and more. This, too, is one of those nonessential issues in the church, but also one that really jumps out at us when we first walk into a church.

I want to encourage you to go into a church with an open mind. In fact, I am going to make the bold statement that an LDS sacrament service, while comfortable to us, really doesn't show a biblical pattern.

Another of my favorite stories in the Old Testament focuses on when King David brought the Ark of the Covenant into Jerusalem. Up to that time, the Ark hadn't had a permanent home, so King David wanted to rectify that. I won't repeat the whole story of what he did, but my favorite part of that story is that when they brought it into the city, King David actually stripped off his robes and danced and sang all the way into the city! (You can read this story in 2 Samuel 6.)

Acts 13:22 tells us that David was a man after God's own heart. I think this whole-hearted worship of God is one of the reasons that God said that about David, and I think it helps us see how God wants us to worship Him—with all of who we are.

A worship service, the part of the service where we sing at a Christian church, really is just that: a worship service. Just as King David did in the Old Testament, our worshipping God might take on the appearance of wholehearted joy with dancing, or deep thoughts with silence, or perhaps even tears of repentance, or somewhere in between. Would it also surprise you to learn that in the Old Testament worship was often accompanied by raised hands as a physical sign of real worship?

All this explanation to say, no matter how the worship service appears to you, give it a chance and really look at what they're singing and how they worship. You might be surprised to learn that many contemporary Christian songs are taken from Psalms.

There are also some other things that you might want to look for when choosing a church. One of them is to look for a church that meets the needs of your family. That means that if you have small children, you'll want to find a church with classes for them. Most churches also have various Bible studies for all ages. For the teenagers, they'll have a youth group. For the women, there will be a ladies' Bible study, and for the men, there will be a men's group of some kind. Often, too, churches will have a "college and career" group for the young single adults, and a senior group as well.

Another trend in Christian churches is to have "small groups." You'll often see this in large churches, but small ones have them too. The idea behind a small group is to get people to develop friendships with others in the church. For that reason, a smaller group usually consisting of five to twenty individuals, will meet together for a time to study the Bible regularly and to pray for one another. These groups are designed to be more like the biblical concept of a house church within the larger church, which meets together to worship corporately.

What kind of groups your church has may be a good reason to consider a church. You will want to go to a church that can minister to all the age groups that your family has. Later on, these ministries will be places that you can help out in too.

Something you can do nowadays that might be a huge help to you would be to check out a church's Website before you go. Doing this might help you to get a "feel" for what is important to that church. It'll also tell you what they believe, which is usually called a Statement of Faith. One thing you can check for is if the church believes those essentials I mentioned above. It may be hard to discern this, but in their Statement of Faith you should be able to see what a church believes. You can always call a church's office or send an e-mail to verify this if you want. The Website could also give you some clues on how their worship services are. For instance, if a church says that they have a contemporary service, that probably means that the people will dress in a more relaxed style, and that the singing will be modern, or contemporary, songs. If it mentions a traditional service, it'll be a bit more formal, and the singing will usually consist of mainly older, traditional hymns (more like you sang as an **LDS** person). You can also check out the photos on the Website. If the photos are of people dressed really casually, rest assured you can leave your tie at home. Very few American churches dress as formally as we did at our **LDS** church. Usually, clean, professional attire is more than good enough for church services.

Another real good approach would be to get a recommendation from a trusted Christian friend. In this way, your friend will pave your way and help you feel welcome right from the start. With us, this happened by my running into my old friend from college. What Sue did that really helped us was to connect us with a wonderful Sunday School class, and the man who was in charge of that class was more than willing to meet with us and discuss our specific questions. He later became one of our closest friends!

Something we did, too, when choosing our first church was to meet with the pastor and head elder, or deacon, of that church. You can ask them all kinds of questions about their church. Honestly, sometimes they didn't answer our questions very well. They simply did not know where we were coming from, since we were looking at things from an **LDS** perspective. However, they did give us a biblical reason for what they believed in. I even asked them why Baptists don't dance, and whether I could continue dancing if I joined their church, and they weren't offended at all.

Lastly, before choosing a church, pray, pray, pray. I mentioned before that our method in choosing our initial church wasn't very scientific. Well, God can and does use our circumstances to direct us, but He's also told us we should pray about everything. Praying about where He'd have you worship is a real good way to start your search. Not that you're doing it like when you were

LDS—to know if this is the true church—but instead humbly showing God that you know He's in control, and that He can and will lead and guide you to the right place for your family.

Know, too, that if you go and don't feel "right" about the church, that's okay. There are many, many Christians who go "church-hopping" before they settle into a new church. It's okay! There's no mandate that you have to be in a certain boundary, or that you have to love everyone in your new church, or even that you have to find a church you're totally comfortable in within the first month. In fact, it'd be real surprising if you were. If you do find a church you like, know that there's no hurry at all to join it. It's more than okay to wait and learn, and watch and see, and make that decision when you feel the time is right for you.

"Not forsaking the assembling of ourselves
together, as the manner of some is;
but exhorting one another:
and so much the more,
as ye see the day approaching. "

— Hebrews 10:25 —

Chapter Seven

WHY GO TO CHURCH AT ALL?

I once knew a man in our ward who came to Sacrament Meeting and then rushed right home afterward, skipping all the other meetings each week. Maybe you've known folks like that as well? Some might have stayed until just after the passing of the sacrament then left right afterward. That's because, as LDS folks, we were taught that it was a commandment to go to church to take the sacrament each week. In fact, it was so important to do, that if someone was very ill and couldn't get to church for a few weeks, someone from the church would bring the sacrament to them. We were taught that we had to do this to be forgiven of our sins each week and prepared to face the next week.

When we look at the Bible, though, the reason for going to church is very different. In fact, we find that receiving the sacrament, or taking communion[1], isn't why we go to church at all. Instead, the reason we go to church is all about relationships. It's about being together with other believers and serving one another. Remember what we learned about what the universal church is, and how it is made up of all believers everywhere? We learned that we are an important part of the body of which Jesus is the head.

We go to church, then, so we can fulfill our role in the body of Christ. Maybe right now you feel that you can't fulfill any kind of role and that you're more like an appendix—something that could be left out and no one would even care. But the truth is that God is working in each and every one of us, and He does have something for you to do, even right now. Note, though, that this doing is not at all like an LDS calling, but instead very possibly might be just saying hi to someone or encouraging someone because you are so excited about God.

Later on, after you've had a chance to grow and understand the Bible better, you might realize you've been given a particular gift. Perhaps it might be teaching, and so you'll exercise that gift by teaching a class. Or it might be the gift of serving, and so you'll be the one in the kitchen serving the pot luck luncheon, or the handyman who no one ever sees but who keeps the church in tip-top shape.

Hebrews 10:25 tells us that we shouldn't forsake assembling together. That's because God knew—planned it even—that each and every one of us has something we can give and receive from one another. We can encourage one another, teach one another, pray for one another, and love one another.

The Bible in several places tells us that the role of a pastor or elder is to teach sound doctrine, ensuring that the church stays on track doctrinally. Because of this, going to church and learning from a pastor or elder will be a great help to you at this stage of your journey. Their teaching will greatly accelerate the process of replacing LDS doctrine with biblical doctrine in your mind.

Know, too, that if you have questions beyond the Sunday services, most pastors and teachers would gladly welcome the chance to meet with you individually to address your questions and concerns. You don't even have to be a member of their church. Attending Sunday School or a small group, as I mentioned previously, are other great venues where you can learn who God is and what He wants from you. These opportunities will help you greatly in your individual study as well as introduce you to gifted teachers who can answer your questions.

> Two are better than one; because they have a good reward for their labour. For if they fall, the one will lift up his fellow: but woe to him that is alone when he falleth; for he hath not another to help him up. Again, if two lie together, then they have heat: but how can one be warm alone? And if one prevail against him, two shall withstand him; and a threefold cord is not quickly broken. (Ecclesiastes 4:9-12)

This passage from Ecclesiastes points out yet another good reason for going to church. We go to encourage one another and, in that process, help one another grow stronger. That's what the body of Christ is all about—encouraging and helping one another.

In addition, as a church, and as individuals within that church, we have a job to do. Jesus' last words tell us that we are to: "Go ye therefore, and teach all nations,…" (Matthew 28:19)

This commandment, commonly referred to as the great commission, was Jesus' last one; and it is the duty of the church everywhere. A good church will teach its members how to tell others about Jesus and will provide ample opportunities to do so, including sending out missionaries to do the job throughout the world to share the gospel in places where not every member of the church can go. As you learn and grow in knowing who Jesus is, you'll want to join in with your local church in accomplishing this task.

To sum it up, our reasons for going to church as a Christian include:

- encouraging one another,
- using our spiritual gifts,
- learning sound doctrine,
- becoming equipped to share our faith, and
- being part of reaching the world for Christ.

"Double, double, toil and trouble," said Shakespeare. Does your life ever feel like that? Mine sure has and often does. To be truthful, many a Sunday I'm tempted to just turn over and go back to bed rather than go to church; and sometimes I do. However, when I make the effort to get myself up, get dressed, and go, I am always blessed, but not in the spiritual sense, although that may happen too. Instead, I'm blessed because someone in the church gives me a hug or shares how God is working in their life, which I could apply directly to myself, or the pastor says something in the message that encourages me, or I'm touched because I took time to lift my voice in praise to God in the midst of the singing. That's what church is all about, you see, encouraging one another in our walk with God. And, it's truly why the smartest being in the universe—God—has said we should go.

[1]Communion, or The Lord's Supper, is what Christians generally call the ceremony of eating bread and drinking wine or grape juice like Jesus did at the last supper. He told us to do this in remembrance of Him. Most Christian churches do this monthly, but some do it less or more than that.

Chapter Eight

WHO AM I?

There's a country music song out titled *Who Am I*, by Jessica Andrews, that describes the song writer's heritage. It says she's so and so's granddaughter, and looks like her father, and her mother's her biggest fan. It then goes on and on with character traits, inherited traits, and developed traits that the songwriter sees in herself.

When you look at yourself, you probably have a similar story: accomplishments you're proud of because you've developed those things, or particular traits you were born with that you like, and maybe some things you don't like about yourself too. The apostle Paul told a similar story in Philippians 3:

> Though I might also have confidence in the flesh.
> If any other man thinketh that he hath whereof
> he might trust in the flesh, I more: Circumcised
> the eighth day, of the stock of Israel, of the tribe of
> Benjamin, an Hebrew of the Hebrews; as touching
> the law, a Pharisee; Concerning zeal, persecuting the

church; touching the righteousness which is in the
law, blameless. (Philippians 3:4-6)

It's an interesting story and tells us right where Paul was before
he knew Christ. An interesting note is what he writes in the very
next verse: "But what things were gain to me, those I counted
loss for Christ." (Philippians 3:7)

When I was LDS, I would have said something like this: "I'm
an eighth-generation Mormon, great-granddaughter of the man
who owned the Manti temple. I'm temple-worthy, do my Family
Home Evening; I'm first counselor in the Young Women's Presi-
dency; I'm a good employee, a mother of five children," and so on.

What I want to talk about now, though, is who we are biblically
or, more accurately, who we are in God's eyes, because that's
the heritage that counts. I think we'll come to see, like Paul, that
all those things we are so proud of are actually nothing when it
comes to knowing Christ.

A widespread belief in Mormonism, and in much of the world,
is that we are children of God. In a general sense, the Bible
does teach that we are children of God. But these references,
upon further study, are used in a way that an inventor might call
something "his baby." We know very well that it's not literally his
baby, but instead is something he poured great effort into and
therefore feels a paternal pride over.

As we study the Bible, we see that we are like the inventor's
creation—God's highest creation—but still His creation. Psalms
139 is perhaps the clearest passage for describing who we are in
relation to God. It says in the King James Version:

I will praise thee; for I am fearfully and wonderfully
made: marvellous are thy works; and that my soul
knoweth right well. My substance was not hid from

thee, when I was made in secret, and curiously wrought in the lowest parts of the earth. Thine eyes did see my substance, yet being unperfect; and in thy book all my members were written, which in continuance were fashioned, when as yet there was none of them. (Psalms 139:14-16 KJV)

The New Century Version of the Bible translates the same passage in a way that's somewhat easier to understand:

I praise you because you made me in an amazing and wonderful way. What you have done is wonderful. I know this very well. You saw my bones being formed as I took shape in my mother's body. When I was put together there, you saw my body as it was formed. All the days planned for me were written in your book before I was one day old. (Psalms 139:14-16 NCV)

Isaiah also talked about God as the Creator of everything, including people. Here are some scriptural examples:

Lift up your eyes on high, and behold who hath created these things, that bringeth out their host by number: he calleth them all by names by the greatness of his might, for that he is strong in power; not one faileth. Why sayest thou, O Jacob, and speakest, O Israel, My way is hid from the LORD, and my judgment is passed over from my God? Hast thou not known? hast thou not heard, that the everlasting God, the LORD, the Creator of the ends of the earth, fainteth not, neither is weary…. (Isaiah 40:26-28)

But now thus saith the LORD that created thee, O Jacob, and he that formed thee, O Israel, Fear not:

for I have redeemed thee, I have called thee by thy
name; thou art mine. (Isaiah 43:1)

Biblically speaking, we're God's creation and not by nature
His children. However, the Bible also teaches that we can become children of God.

But as many as received him, to them gave he power
to become the sons of God, even to them that believe
on his name: (John 1:12)

We do this by being adopted by God.

But when the fullness of the time was come, God sent
forth his Son, made of a woman, made under the law,
To redeem them that were under the law, that we
might receive the adoption of sons. (Galatians 4:4-5)

Behold, what manner of love the Father hath bestowed upon us, that we should be called the sons of
God: therefore the world knoweth us not, because
it knew him not. Beloved, now are we the sons of
God,…. (1 John 3:1-2)

Having predestinated us unto the adoption of children by Jesus Christ to himself, according to the good
pleasure of his will,….(Ephesians 1:5)

For as many as are led by the Spirit of God, they
are the sons of God. For ye have not received the
spirit of bondage again to fear; but ye have received
the Spirit of adoption, whereby we cry, Abba, Father.
(Romans 8:14-15)

Again, the first thing we must know about ourselves is that we
are God's creation, and that we have the possibility of becoming
adopted sons and daughters of God.

Next, another underlying principle of the Bible we need to

understand is that we're sinners and separated from a holy God. On the surface that seems somewhat obvious. Who among us hasn't seen that we sin? I for one can see my sin, and I suspect that you can, too, if you're honest with yourself. Biblical sin, on the other hand, is much deeper than that. It is rooted in our deepest, darkest nature.

Genesis 2 and 3 explain how this came to be:

And the LORD God took the man, and put him into the garden of Eden to dress it and to keep it. And the LORD God commanded the man, saying, "Of every tree of the garden thou mayest freely eat: But of the tree of the knowledge of good and evil, thou shalt not eat of it: for in the day that thou eatest thereof thou shalt surely die." (Genesis 2:15-17)

Now the serpent was more subtil than any beast of the field which the LORD God had made. And he said unto the woman, "Yea, hath God said, Ye shall not eat of every tree of the garden?" And the woman said unto the serpent, "We may eat of the fruit of the trees of the garden: But of the fruit of the tree which is in the midst of the garden, God hath said, 'Ye shall not eat of it, neither shall ye touch it, lest ye die.'" And the serpent said unto the woman, "Ye shall not surely die: For God doth know that in the day ye eat thereof, then your eyes shall be opened, and ye shall be as gods, knowing good and evil." And when the woman saw that the tree was good for food, and that it was pleasant to the eyes, and a tree to be desired to make one

wise, she took of the fruit thereof, and did eat, and
gave also unto her husband with her; and he did
eat. And the eyes of them both were opened, and
they knew that they were naked; and they sewed
fig leaves together, and made themselves aprons.
(Genesis 3:1-7)

I quote this in its entirety here because if you're like me, you've
heard this particular story a million times. You've heard it in
Sunday School, in Primary, in the temple, or read it once or
twice yourself, and so forth. But this time I'm asking you to read
it without the unique LDS beliefs attached to it, and see what
God actually says.

Here are a couple of points I want you to note:

- The first thing Satan does is question God's Word and
  change God's Word. In chapter 3, verse 1 he says, "Yea,
  hath God said, Ye shall not eat of every tree of the garden?" This is a trick that Satan has used throughout
  history and continues to use even to this day. Eve buys
  into it by adding even more to what God had said. In
  verse 3, note her addition of "neither shall you touch it."

- Notice what Satan promises Eve—the possibility of becoming a God, as stated in verse 5, chapter 3 "…and
  ye shall be as gods,…" This, too, is a trick that Satan
  uses even to this day to entice us.

Then we see God's reaction to Adam and Eve's sin:

And they heard the voice of the LORD God walking in the garden in the cool of the day: and Adam
and his wife hid themselves from the presence of the
LORD God amongst the trees of the garden. And
the LORD God called unto Adam, and said unto

him, "Where art thou?" And he said, "I heard thy voice in the garden, and I was afraid, because I was naked; and I hid myself." And he said, "Who told thee that thou wast naked? Hast thou eaten of the tree, whereof I commanded thee that thou shouldest not eat?" And the man said, "The woman whom thou gavest to be with me, she gave me of the tree, and I did eat."

And the LORD God said unto the woman, "What is this that thou hast done?" And the woman said, "The serpent beguiled me, and I did eat." And the LORD God said unto the serpent, "Because thou hast done this, thou art cursed above all cattle, and above every beast of the field; upon thy belly shalt thou go, and dust shalt thou eat all the days of thy life: And I will put enmity between thee and the woman, and between thy seed and her seed; it shall bruise thy head, and thou shalt bruise his heel." Unto the woman he said, "I will greatly multiply thy sorrow and thy conception; in sorrow thou shalt bring forth children; and thy desire shall be to thy husband, and he shall rule over thee." And unto Adam he said, "Because thou hast hearkened unto the voice of thy wife, and hast eaten of the tree, of which I commanded thee, saying, Thou shalt not eat of it: cursed is the ground for thy sake; in sorrow shalt thou eat of it all the days of thy life; Thorns also and thistles shall it bring forth to thee; and thou shalt eat the herb of the field; In the sweat of thy face shalt thou eat bread, till thou return unto the ground; for out of it wast thou taken:

for dust thou art, and unto dust shalt thou return." And Adam called his wife's name Eve; because she was the mother of all living. Unto Adam also and to his wife did the **LORD** God make coats of skins, and clothed them. And the **LORD** God said, "Behold, the man is become as one of us, to know good and evil: and now, lest he put forth his hand, and take also of the tree of life, and eat, and live for ever: Therefore the **LORD** God sent him forth from the garden of Eden, to till the ground from whence he was taken." So he drove out the man; and he placed at the east of the garden of Eden Cherubims, and a flaming sword which turned every way, to keep the way of the tree of life. (Genesis 3:8-24)

We can learn a number of lessons from this passage, but right now I'd like you to note three:

1. No matter how you look at it, Adam and Eve sinned against God. He gave a commandment, and they chose, deliberately, to disobey it. Disobeying God is a sin no matter how much justification we might think there might be.

2. Because of Adam and Eve's sin, they were separated spiritually from God. Scripture refers to this separation as death. Adam and Eve were spiritually separated from God right away, and later when their lives would be over, they would physically be separated from God by death. From this point on, all of mankind inherited Adam's propensity to sin—or sinful, separated-from-God nature.

3. In verse 8, note that God came looking for Adam

and Eve. Apparently, walking with them in the cool of the day was a habit—something God did with them regularly. Then in verses 23 and 24, we see that God sent them out, or drove them out, of His presence. They no longer regularly walked with God because they were separated from him spiritually, or were spiritually dead.

This separation from God, caused by man's propensity to sin, or sinful nature, is mankind's fundamental problem and underlies everything the Bible teaches from Genesis 3 onward. Here are a few other verses that talk about this problem:

Behold, I was shapen in iniquity; and in sin did my mother conceive me. (Psalms 51:5)

Wherefore, as by one man sin entered into the world, and death by sin; and so death passed upon all men, for that all have sinned:… Therefore as by the offence of one judgment came upon all men to condemnation;. . . For as by one man's disobedience many were made sinners,… (Romans 5:12, 18-19)

In reality, we've inherited our propensity to sin from our grandfather, Adam. It's truly part of the human nature. So the second thing we need to know about ourselves, from a biblical perspective, is that we are sinners by nature. In other words, we sin because it's in our very nature. Romans 3 expounds on this lesson by quoting from several Psalms:

As it is written, There is none righteous, no, not one: There is none that understandeth, there is none that seeketh after God. They are all gone out of the way, they are together become unprofitable; there is none that doeth good, no, not one. Their throat is an open sepulchre; with their tongues they have used deceit; the poison of asps is under their lips: Whose mouth is full of cursing and bitterness: Their feet are swift to shed blood: Destruction and misery are in their ways: And the way of peace have they not known: There is no fear of God before their eyes... For all have sinned, and come short of the glory of God; (Romans 3:10-18, 23)

To summarize this particular passage, note the following:

- None of us are righteous.
- None of us, left to ourselves, seeks after God.
- None of us does good—really.
- Destruction and misery are the way of mankind. We do not know how to make real and lasting peace with God.
- We all sin and come short of God's glory.

For me, this concept was a hard one to swallow. I, probably like you, always considered myself a good person. Oh, I wasn't perfect, but on the scale of human badness, I hadn't done anything real bad. I wasn't an adulterer, I wasn't a murderer, and I hadn't been to jail for anything or even been picked up by the police, although I did have a few speeding tickets. I had never seriously hurt my children in any way. I hadn't stole, I hadn't cheated, and I hadn't lied—well, most of the time. When I heard terms like *total depravity*, I fought strenuously against that idea because, when I heard "depravity," I thought of a serial killer who ate the flesh of his victims instead of realizing what it really meant, which was that I was a sinner separated from a Holy God. Nonetheless, the biblical truth is that, in God's eyes, I was a sinner. I had committed adultery in my heart when I looked at a man with lustful thoughts. I had committed murder in my heart when I screamed and yelled, even silently, at the driver who cut me off. I had lied from time to time to get what I wanted or to avoid problems. I had robbed Him by not giving when I should have, and so on. The bottom line is that I hadn't obeyed God like I should have.

Think about it for just a minute. I bet you might have a similar list or maybe one not as long as mine or, then again, worse than mine. At this point, don't worry about your list too much. Just know that this is who God says you are—a sinner. And because you're a sinner, you're separated from a Holy God.

To recap, up to this point we've learned that:

> 1. God created us, and we're not yet His children but instead have the potential of being adopted by Him to become His children.
>
> 2. We're sinners who are separated from God.

The next thing that's important for us to realize is that we can't do anything that will pay for our sin. Generally, I think most people believe that their good and bad works somehow balance out as in a scale. In other words, when they do enough good, it somehow balances out their sin, Therefore, when they die and that balance is still for the positive, they believe God will look at that and accept them.

In their view, going to heaven somehow looks like this scale:

Good Works   *Bad Works*

Or I suppose what they're hoping for looks more like this: their good works on the upside, and their bad works, or sins, on the downside.

Good Works   *Bad Works*

Mormonism views justice this way, except it throws in Jesus "after all we can do." In effect, this means that whether your scale looks like either of the scales above, Jesus will come and put his hand on the good side and therefore help you out.

The Bible, however, tells a slightly different story. It tells us that our "good works" are worth nothing when it comes to earning the right to be the children of God. In fact, it tells us they are worse than nothing, and actually are as "filthy rags" in God's sight. The Hebrew word translated to mean filthy rags actually describes dirty, stinking, menstrual rags—good for nothing at all except to throw away. Here's the verse that talks about filthy rags:

> But we are all as an unclean thing, and all our righteousnesses are as filthy rags; and we all do fade as a leaf; and our iniquities, like the wind, have taken us away. (Isaiah 64:6)

We can see, according to the Bible, that our scale system is in big trouble. Our "good works" that we were counting on to help us in balancing our scale are actually now on the "bad" side, and we haven't a hope. We are completely and totally lost in our attempt to reach God. In fact, we're looking something like this:

Good Works   *Bad Works*

And that's the picture the Bible paints. Listen to these words from Paul to the church at Ephesus describing how they had lived before they put their faith in Jesus:

> Wherein in time past ye walked according to the course of this world, according to the prince of the power of the air, the spirit that now worketh in the children of disobedience: Among whom also we all had our conversation in times past in the lusts of our flesh, fulfilling the desires of the flesh and of the mind; and were by nature the children of wrath, even as others…. (Ephesians 2:2-3)

He says nearly the same thing to the church in Colossae:

> And you, being dead in your sins and the uncircumcision of your flesh,… (Colossians 2:13)

Now let's look once again at who we are biblically. The picture is starting to come together and, honestly, it's not a pretty picture:

> 1. I'm God's creation—His special creation—the one He put together in a very special way.
>
> 2. I'm a wicked, ugly sinner who is separated from God by my sin.
>
> 3. I can't do anything good enough to reconcile myself to God, or even please God, no matter how wonderful my good works and no matter how obedient I am.

Pretty grim, isn't it? I started this chapter with a song describing who I was. I want to finish with a line from an old hymn that hits the nail on the head when it comes to describing who we all are:

> Sorrowing I shall be in spirit, 'till released from flesh and sin…prone to wander, Lord, I feel it, prone to leave the God I love; (*Come Thou Fount of Every Blessing, Robert Robinson*)

Before I close with such grim news, let me point out that Jesus does hold the answer to our sin problem. He is truly the Good News! We are not left to be who we are by nature, but instead Jesus will make us into who He wants us to be. He has a plan for us—a perfect plan—and He wants us to join Him in that plan. Praise the God of Heaven for His solution to our problem. But before I go there, I want first to explore who is this God, and who is Jesus. Just like it was important to see who we are biblically, it's just as important to see who God—the only true God—is.

Chapter Nine

WHO IS GOD?

Throughout the years, Hollywood has made various movies that showed us pictures of God. In one movie from my youth, yes, I'm that old, George Burns played God. For those who haven't seen, *Oh God,* George Burns played God and depicted Him as a slightly lecherous, but loveable, cigar-smoking old man. More recently, Morgan Freeman played God in the movie, *Bruce Almighty.* In this movie, Morgan Freeman portrayed God more conservatively, but as an older gentleman of African American descent who seemed both wise and kind.

Now for those of us in American culture, and especially LDS culture, we've seen God depicted our entire lives as a fiftyish man with long brown hair, a beard, and mustache, and surrounded by light. It's an image that reminds us of our kindly grandfather or a favorite wise uncle.

The question, of course, that begs to be asked is: "Is that God?" And, "What is God like, really? Is He benevolent, or a dictator?

Is He love, or is He justice? Is He white or black, brown-skinned, or with Israeli type features? Or could He look Asian?"

That's what I want to talk about now. But before we start, let me just say that this particular topic is huge—so huge that you'll never, ever quit studying it—honestly. Because God is BIG—way, way bigger than our finite minds can understand. And, I'm not even going to try to describe everything about God, but instead am going to concentrate on things that you might not understand—things that you need to understand to know who the God of the Bible is.

You probably already know quite a bit about God. For instance, you probably know that God is all-powerful, or omnipotent, and all knowing, or omniscient. And, you probably even know that God is everywhere all the time, or omnipresent. You also probably know that God is love, and that God is just.

I'm not going to spend a lot of time talking about these particular attributes, but instead want to talk about the attributes of God that Mormonism teaches that are different from what the Bible teaches. To start, let's look at what God is like physically.

Going back to the movies I mentioned, is He the slightly lecherous but loveable old white guy, or the wise and handsome black man? Or is He truthfully somewhere in between?

The Psalms describe God more than any other book, and they should be our first place to study if we want to really know who God is. Psalms 18 says the following about God:

> The LORD is my rock, and my fortress, and my deliverer; my God, my strength, in whom I will trust; my buckler, and the horn of my salvation, and my high tower…In my distress I called upon the LORD, and cried unto my God: he heard my voice out of

his temple, and my cry came before him, even into his ears. Then the earth shook and trembled; the foundations also of the hills moved and were shaken, because he was wroth. There went up a smoke out of his nostrils, and fire out of his mouth devoured: coals were kindled by it. He bowed the heavens also, and came down: and darkness was under his feet. And he rode upon a cherub, and did fly: yea, he did fly upon the wings of the wind…The LORD also thundered in the heavens, and the Highest gave his voice; hail stones and coals of fire…and he shot out lightnings, and discomfited them. Then the channels of waters were seen, and the foundations of the world were discovered at thy rebuke, O LORD, at the blast of the breath of thy nostrils…For thou wilt light my candle: the LORD my God will enlighten my darkness…As for God, his way is perfect: the word of the LORD is tried: he is a buckler to all those that trust in him. For who is God save the LORD? or who is a rock save our God? (Psalms 18:2, 6-10, 13, 15, 28, 30-31)

This Psalm illustrates the first characteristic that's vitally important for us to understand about God—that He is not a man. He's infinitely above us in power, in strength, and in imagination, so much so that we can't even hope to grasp fully who He is. This Psalm shows His amazing power, but there are other verses where God speaks directly to us saying very clearly that He is not a man, like Isaiah 11:9, " … for I am God, and not man;…" or Psalms 50:21, which says:

These things hast thou done, and I kept silence; thou thoughtest that I was altogether such an one as

thyself: but I will reprove thee, and set them in order
before thine eyes.

In these passages, God is quite explicit that He is absolutely
not a man. LDS doctrine, as you know, says that God was a man
who worked His way up to become a God by becoming better
and better, somehow, and in some way, until He achieved god-
hood. Joseph Smith also taught that we could someday become
a god just like God became a god. But that's not at all what the
Bible teaches about God. Instead, the Bible teaches that God
was always God, and will always be God—that He's God eternally. "God is a Spirit: and they that worship him must worship
him in spirit and in truth." (John 4:24)

The bottom line is that biblically we don't have any idea what
God actually looks like. We know that Jesus was "God with us"
or, in other words, God in the flesh (See Matthew 1:23 and John
1:1.) We'll study this concept more in the chapter titled "Three
God's, One God, What in the World?" We know, too, that scriptures give us word pictures to help us understand how God cares
for us. Those word pictures include body parts, but don't necessarily mean that God has those body parts. Instead, God is like
mankind in that He hears, moves, speaks, and so on. Here are
some examples of those word pictures I'm talking about. Take
note, though, that not all of the word pictures in scripture describe a human form of nature, but some depict a form of birds,
towers, light, and more—objects clearly not human in nature.

> He shall cover thee with his feathers, and under his
> wings shalt thou trust: (Psalms 91:4; 61:4; 63:7; 57:1;
> and 36:7)

> By the word of the LORD were the heavens made;
> and all the host of them by the breath of his mouth....

The LORD looketh from heaven; (Psalms 33:6, 13)
…by the word of thy lips I have kept me from the
paths of the destroyer. (Psalms 17:4)
The LORD is my light and my salvation.… Hide not
thy face far from me; (Psalms 27:1, 9)

It is also true that God created us "in His image." This truth seems on the surface to be a bit confusing, since on the one hand we know that God is not really like us and we've learned that God is spirit, which would mean He doesn't have a body of flesh and blood like ours. But on the other hand, when we think about it, we are separated from all the rest of creation in our ability to think and reason, and to have a conscience. And that's just what scripture seems to be saying when it says we were created in His image, not a physical resemblance per se, but rather a creation with the ability to think, to reason, and to know right from wrong.

To recap what we've learned so far:

- God is separate from us—above us,
- God is greater than us, and not a human or even an exalted human,
- And God is spirit.

Another thing to know about God is that He's eternal. This, too, is very hard to grasp. I don't know about you, but honestly my brain can't even wrap itself around the idea of eternity—a time without end and without beginning. I think that's normal for all of us. Everything in our world started at some time, and will end at some time. So, to think of a God who is eternal—who has no beginning and no end—is in many ways unfathomable. But that's just what scripture tells us about God. In fact, in scripture we see that God is outside of time—He's not bound by time.

That's because He is actually the Creator of time. Here are just a few verses that point out God's eternality:

> And Abraham planted a grove in Beersheba, and called there on the name of the LORD, the everlasting God. (Genesis 21:33)
>
> The eternal God is thy refuge, and underneath are the everlasting arms:… (Deuteronomy 33:27)
>
> Before the mountains were brought forth, or ever thou hadst formed the earth and the world, even from everlasting to everlasting, thou art God. (Psalms 90:2)
>
> Now unto the King eternal, immortal, invisible, the only wise God, be honour and glory for ever and ever. Amen. (1 Timothy 1:17)
>
> For unto us a child is born, unto us a son is given: and the government shall be upon his shoulder: and his name shall be called… The everlasting Father…, (Isaiah 9:6)

These are not all the verses that call God everlasting, but are only a few of them. As I mentioned before, the LDS Heavenly Father wasn't always God but instead was a man who did good things and eventually was so exalted that he became God. This is not at all how scriptures describe the God of the Bible. Instead, scriptures quite clearly depict God to be The God of all creation from forever and to forever. He is eternally God.

Scriptures also say that God is the Creator of everything, whereas LDS doctrine says that God "organized" matter that was already created. This is important to note, because the God we see in the Bible is so much bigger than what we had imagined. He's big enough, in fact, that Christians throughout the centu-

ries have asserted that He created the world from nothing at all. In fact, the Bible teaches that He spoke, and it was created. Now that's power!

> In the beginning God created the heaven and the earth.… And God said, "Let there be light:" and there was light.… And God said,… And God said,… (Genesis 1:1, 3, 6, 9)
>
> Let them praise the name of the LORD: for he commanded, and they were created. (Psalms 148:5)
>
> I have made the earth, and created man upon it: I, even my hands, have stretched out the heavens, and all their host have I commanded. (Isaiah 45:12)
>
> Thou art worthy, O Lord, to receive glory and honour and power: for thou hast created all things, and for thy pleasure they are and were created. (Revelation 4:11)

Another aspect we should understand about God is that He doesn't change. This is important because, when we look at the Old Testament, we should see the same God as we see today. And when we accept what the Bible alone teaches, we do see the same God throughout history.

> Every good gift and every perfect gift is from above, and cometh down from the Father of lights, with whom is no variableness, neither shadow of turning. (James 1:17)
>
> For I am the LORD, I change not;… (Malachi 3:6)

Lastly, know that in the Old Testament, God gave Moses a very special name by which He could be called. This name was I AM. (See Exodus 3:14.) I bring up this name, because it means a whole lot more than those two words alone convey to us. It means that God is The All-Sufficient being. It means that God doesn't need anything—He doesn't need food to eat, He doesn't need water to drink, He doesn't need oxygen to breathe, He doesn't need an atmosphere to keep him from getting sun-burned, and He doesn't need a jacket to keep Him warm from the cold. He needs nothing at all. He, by Himself, can survive, and live, and thrive without anything else at all. Stop just a moment and think about that—it's somewhat of a mind-blowing concept, isn't it? Ultimately, that is the God the Bible describes, a God who is bigger, and greater, and more powerful, and even more awe-inspiring than anything we can imagine.

I have a good friend who counsels ex-Mormons, and one of the things she tells them is that someday their God is going to get big—real big. And when He does, they'll be blown away. For me, it wasn't until I'd been out a few years and had been studying about who God was in Bible School when this revelation hit me. And it was true: one day in my mind, my image of God grew until He was amazingly big. And I was literally blown away to see how really and truly big God is.

I suppose the reason that happens to us is that, while LDS, we put God in a certain box—a box that was man-sized, big man-sized, certainly. We saw him as being a much more evolved man than any of us. Still, we brought God down to being nothing more than an exalted man. The Bible testifies again and again that God is not, nor ever was a man, but instead has been God from eternity to eternity. It says that God is spirit, and that in many ways we cannot understand Him. It says that He's eternal and that He's eternally been God, and that because He is God, He chose to create our world and us. It's pretty amazing to con-template, and it's why the Psalmists spent all of their time prais-

ing a God who is worthy of all our praise. They truly saw, and worshipped, a BIG God.

> The LORD reigneth; let the people tremble: he sitteth between the cherubims; let the earth be moved. The LORD is great in Zion; and he is high above all the people. Let them praise thy great and terrible name; for it is holy. (Psalms 99:1-3)
>
> The hills melted like wax at the presence of the LORD, at the presence of the Lord of the whole earth. The heavens declare his righteousness, and all the people see his glory. (Psalms 97:5-7)
>
> For the LORD is great, and greatly to be praised: he is to be feared above all gods. Honour and majesty are before him: strength and beauty are in his sanctuary. Give unto the LORD, O ye kindreds of the people, give unto the LORD glory and strength. Give unto the LORD the glory due unto his name: bring an offering, and come into his courts. O worship the LORD in the beauty of holiness: fear before him, all the earth (Psalms 96:4, 6-9)
>
> Praise ye the LORD. O give thanks unto the LORD; for he is good: for his mercy endureth for ever. Who can utter the mighty acts of the LORD? who can shew forth all his praise? (Psalms 106:1-2)

"When Jesus came into the coasts
of Caesarea Philippi, he asked his disciples,
saying, 'Whom do men say that I
the Son of man am ?'"
— Matthew 16:13 —

WHO IS JESUS?

ne day when Jesus was walking with his disciples, He asked them an interesting question: "Whom do men say that I the Son of man am?" One of them answered, "They think you're John the Baptist." Another one answered and said, "They think you're one of the prophets, like Elias." And yet another answered and said, "They think you're Jeremiah."

Then Jesus asked the most important question of all: "But who do you think that I am?" Scripture records that Peter answered: "Thou art the Christ, the Son of the living God." (See Matthew 16:13-16.) Jesus then congratulated Peter for his answer and told him that God Himself had revealed that information to him.

That particular question that Jesus asked is as important today as it was in that day. Who is Jesus? More importantly: "…But whom say ye that I am?" (Jesus, from Matthew 16.)

Who do we believe that Jesus is?

In the LDS church, we were taught that Jesus was our older brother and was born as the first spirit-child of God, and that you and I were born somewhere down the line as the 29,345 billionth, give or take a few billion. We were also taught that somehow he was a god and had participated in a council of gods in creating the earth. We were taught, more or less, that Jesus was the God of the Old Testament and the God of this world. Overall, we were taught the biblical stories of his birth, his life, and his death on the cross, as well as his subsequent resurrection on the third day.

I don't want to spend a lot of time talking about those biblical events, because we already know about them. But I do want to point out some things the Bible has to say about Jesus that don't quite fit the LDS mold. I think they're very important. In fact, I believe that to put our faith in Jesus as our Savior, we HAVE to know that He is worthy of our faith. And, until we know who Jesus is, we really can't put our faith in Him. Since the Bible says that this is the only way to enter God's presence, it's vitally important that we come to see who Jesus is, biblically.

To start, let's look at some of the prophecies about Jesus found in the Old Testament. Here's one:

> For unto us a child is born, unto us a son is given: and the government shall be upon his shoulder: and his name shall be called Wonderful, Counsellor, The mighty God, The everlasting Father, The Prince of Peace. Of the increase of his government and peace there shall be no end, upon the throne of David, and upon his kingdom, to order it, and to establish it with judgment and with justice from henceforth even for ever. The zeal of the LORD of hosts will perform this. (Isaiah 9:6, 7)

In this prophecy about Jesus' birth, Jesus is described by a number of titles. If you're like me, you're familiar with this prophecy through *Handel's Messiah*. And, if you're like me again, you might never have noticed the significance of what these names mean. Literally, they are Jesus' titles:

- Wonderful
- Counselor, or some translations use the first two together, as Wonderful Counselor
- The Mighty God
- The Everlasting Father
- The Prince of Peace

In addition, you might never have noticed that Jesus' names include the Mighty God or the Everlasting Father. So the first titles for Jesus I want to point out are that He is:

- the Mighty God, and
- the Everlasting Father.

Let's look at another of those prophecies about Jesus to discover more about who He really is:

> Therefore the Lord himself shall give you a sign; Behold, a virgin shall conceive, and bear a son, and shall call his name Immanuel. (Isaiah 7:14)
>
> Behold, a virgin shall be with child, and shall bring forth a son, and they shall call his name Emmanuel, which being interpreted is, God with us. (Matthew 1:23)

Maybe you had also never noticed that this particular prophecy says that Jesus is quite literally, "God with us."

Let's add that to our list:

- Jesus is the Mighty God,
- Jesus is the Everlasting Father, and
- Jesus is God with us.

Stick with me now while I explain why I believe this particular title is important. First, if Jesus were only our older brother, like we're told he is in LDS teaching, and even if he were that older brother who was almost, or just about, a god, he really wouldn't be worthy of saving us.

Think back at what we learned about ourselves—who we are as human beings—how we have all sinned (Romans 3:23) and can't even do righteous things on our own (Isaiah 64:6.) If Jesus was just like us in every way—a man, there's no way he could have done anything righteous enough to take away our sins. He would have been under the same limitations, and sin, as the rest of us are, but that's not what the Bible teaches about Jesus. Instead, the Bible teaches that Jesus, while being 100 percent man, was also 100 percent God—God with us. John tells us this truth quite plainly in chapter one, verse one, of his gospel: "In the beginning was the Word, and the Word was with God, and the Word was God."

Theologians call this union between God and the man Jesus the hypostatic union. The reason this is important to understand is that only Jesus, since He was God, could take away our sins. As God, He qualified as our Savior and Redeemer.

> Neither is there salvation in any other: for there is none other name under heaven given among men, whereby we must be saved. (Acts 4:12)
>
> Jesus saith unto him, "I am the way, the truth, and the life: no man cometh unto the Father, but by me." (John 14:6)

Here we learn another important fact about Jesus. He is the way to God. In other words, God has said that if we want to come to Him and be saved and have eternal life with Him forever, we have to do it through Jesus. We'll talk more about this in another chapter, but for now it's important to note that Jesus is the way to God.

Let's recap what we've learned about Jesus so far:
- Jesus is the Mighty God;
- Jesus is the Everlasting Father;
- Jesus is God with us;
- Jesus is God;
- Jesus was fully human and fully God; and
- Jesus is the way we come to the Father.

Another important fact the Bible teaches about Jesus is that He, too, is eternal, just like God the Father. In John 17, while Jesus was praying to God the Father, He reveals His eternality: "And now, O Father, glorify thou me with thine own self with the glory which I had with thee before the world was." (John 17:5)

This scripture, combined with John 1:1, shows us that Jesus had always been with God and that like God, He also is not a created being, unlike us. Hebrews 13:8 clarifies that truth when it tells us that Jesus is the same and has never, changed. It says: "Jesus Christ the same yesterday, and to day, and for ever."

It's also interesting to note that Jesus calls Himself the self-existent one, or the one who needs nothing more to exist—just like God.

> "Your father Abraham rejoiced to see my day: and he saw it, and was glad." Then said the Jews unto him, "Thou art not yet fifty years old, and hast thou seen Abraham?" Jesus said unto them, "Verily, verily, I say unto you, Before Abraham was, I am." Then took they up stones to cast at him: but Jesus hid himself, and went out of the temple, going through the midst of them, and so passed by. (John 8:56-59)

In this passage, Jesus makes a very clear reference as far back as Exodus 3:14, when God said that He was the I AM. The people of that day also understood that He was equating Himself with God, which is why they tried to stone Him. So when we think of Jesus, we need to know that the Bible teaches that He is self-existent and has always existed, just as God the Father has always existed.

In addition, the Bible teaches that it was Jesus who created the world:

> For by him were all things created, that are in heaven, and that are in earth, visible and invisible, whether they be thrones, or dominions, or principalities, or powers: all things were created by him, and for him: And he is before all things, and by him all things consist. (Colossians 1:16-17)
>
> Hath in these last days spoken unto us by his Son, whom he hath appointed heir of all things, by whom also he made the worlds; (Hebrews 1:2)

Scripture also teaches that Jesus is of a higher rank than the angels.[1] Therefore, He's not an angel. "Being made so much better than the angels," (Hebrews 1:4 referring to Jesus)

"And again, when he bringeth in the first begotten into the world, he saith, And let all the angels of God worship him." (Hebrews 1:6)

Another important fact about Jesus is that He is higher than any of God's creation. In fact, one day all of creation will fall at His feet and worship Him.

> Wherefore God also hath highly exalted him, and given him a name which is above every name: That at the name of Jesus every knee should bow, of things in heaven, and things in earth, and things under the earth; And that every tongue should confess that Jesus Christ is Lord, to the glory of God the Father. (Philippians 2:9-11)

Who Is Jesus?

After Jesus' resurrection, the disciples openly worshipped Him, and He did not correct them or tell them not to do so:

> In the end of the sabbath, as it began to dawn toward the first day of the week, came Mary Magdalene and the other Mary to see the sepulchre…. He is not here: for he is risen, as he said…. And as they went to tell his disciples, behold, Jesus met them, saying, All hail. And they came and held him by the feet, and worshipped him. Then said Jesus unto them, Be not afraid: go tell my brethren that they go into Galilee, and there shall they see me. (Matthew 28:1, 6-10)

To recap just a bit, let's look at who, so far, the Bible says that Jesus is:

First we learned that Jesus is called:

- Wonderful,
- Counselor,
- The Mighty God,
- The Everlasting Father,
- The Prince of Peace.

And that Jesus is:

- God with us,
- God, and
- The only way that we can come to God.

We've also learned that He:

- existed with God in the beginning,
- is eternal,
- is self-existent,
- is much greater than the angels,
- is higher than any other creation, and
- indeed is the Creator of the Universe.

Note that after His resurrection, God exalted Jesus to His right hand, and from there He lives to intercede for us daily.

> Who is he that condemneth? It is Christ that died, yea rather, that is risen again, who is even at the right hand of God, who also maketh intercession for us. (Romans 8:34)

> Wherefore he is able also to save them to the uttermost that come unto God by him, seeing he ever liveth to make intercession for them. (Hebrews 7:25)

Scripture also tells us that Jesus is the head of the church today. (See Colossians 1:18.)

Prophecy tells us that Jesus is going to come in the last days as the conquering Messiah who will slay armies larger than any that had ever been on this earth just by breathing on them. The book of Revelation talks about this aspect of Jesus. For now, though, it's enough to know that sometime in the future, Jesus will be coming back as our conquering king.

The Bible tells us that when Jesus was here on earth, He was fulfilling a prophecy that God had planned right from the very beginning of time. Before closing this topic, let's look a bit more closely at what, in the LDS church, we referred to as the Atonement.

Once a year in ancient Israel, the Israelites enacted a ritual that symbolized what Jesus would do when He was here. It happened on the Day of Atonement, known as Yom Kippur in Hebrew. What happened on that day was that the high priest laid his hands on an animal, symbolically transferring all the sins of the people onto the animal. Then, that animal was killed and its blood collected.

Next, the high priest went into the Holy of Holies. Inside were the Ark of the Covenant and the mercy seat. Once inside, the

high priest sprinkled the blood all around. No one else but the high priest was allowed into the Holy of Holies, and he was allowed to enter only on this one day every year. By way of this ritual, the people's sins were atoned. It was as though their sins were covered, and God couldn't see them anymore because of the atoning animal's blood. However, since the people's sins were only covered, and not really dealt with, the priest had to come back and perform this ceremony year after year from the time of Moses clear down to Jesus' time.

Several things about Jesus' crucifixion fit this symbolism perfectly, which is how God planned it, of course. First, Jesus died and shed His blood on the cross. This event was absolutely necessary because as scripture says, without shed blood there could be no remission of sin (see Hebrews 9:22). There is no biblical indication that any sacrifice for sin happened in the Garden of Gethsemane. In fact, Moses lifting up his staff to save Israel from snakes, as Jesus referred to in John 3:14, clearly symbolizes that crucifixion was the only way this sacrifice could have taken place. Second, immediately after Jesus died, the veil of the temple that separated the Holy of Holies from the more common portions of the temple was ripped in two from top to bottom. Remember, this was the veil that only the high priest could enter through, and then only once a year. The veil was a very thick cloth. Most accounts say it was a hands-width thick, meaning that there was no way it could have been torn accidentally. Instead, it was obvious to all that this occurrence was supernatural. God ripping the veil supernaturally was another clear sign that the way into the Holy of Holies had been opened up for all men to enter into by Jesus death.

The LDS church teaches that Jesus' sacrifice meant that all of mankind could be resurrected, but there's no reference specifically to that in scripture. Instead, the assumption of scripture was, and always has been, that men would die, be resurrected, and then be judged. We see this taught in the book of Job, considered the oldest book in the Bible by most biblical scholars, by Isaiah several hundred years before Jesus, in Hannah's praise to God for giving her a son before the time of King David, and in other references as well.

> The LORD killeth, and maketh alive: he bringeth
> down to the grave, and bringeth up. (1 Samual 2:6)
> And though after my skin worms destroy this body,
> yet in my flesh shall I see God:... (Job 19:26)
> Thy dead men shall live, together with my dead body
> shall they arise. Awake and sing, ye that dwell in dust:
> for thy dew is as the dew of herbs, and the earth shall
> cast out the dead. (Isaiah 26:19)

Last, the LDS church teaches that Jesus' sacrifice covers our sins after we've done our level best. In other words, we have to try our best, do what we can, live out the ordinances set forth by Jesus, and then His sacrifice kicks in. The Bible, on the other hand, doesn't teach that at all. It teaches, instead, that by splitting the veil in two, God symbolized that all of mankind can come to Him. Indeed, there is no longer a need for a high priest to come in year after year to make atonement. Rather, when Jesus died, all sins whether past, present, or future were paid for.

I'll share more detail about this in another chapter. For now, I want to share what the Bible has to say about Jesus' payment for sin and how it opened the way for us to have free access into the presence of God.

> Wherefore he is able also to save them to the utter-
> most that come unto God by him, seeing he ever

liveth to make intercession for them. For such an high priest became us, who is holy, harmless, undefiled, separate from sinners, and made higher than the heavens; Who needeth not daily, as those high priests, to offer up sacrifice, first for his own sins, and then for the people's: for this he did once, when he offered up himself. (Hebrews 7:25-27)

Therefore being justified by faith, we have peace with God through our Lord Jesus Christ: By whom also we have access by faith into this grace wherein we stand, and rejoice in hope of the glory of God....

But God commendeth his love toward us, in that, while we were yet sinners, Christ died for us.. . . For if, when we were enemies, we were reconciled to God by the death of his Son, much more, being reconciled, we shall be saved by his life. (Romans 5:1,2, 8, and 10)

When I was still LDS, I'd hear songs like the one I'm quoting below and wonder about what it was saying. Truly, I just didn't understand why Christians spent so much time talking about, and singing praise to, Jesus. The truth was, though, that the Jesus I believed in wasn't worthy of that kind of praise. He was, after all, a man ahead of me in progression. He was certainly to be thanked, and I owed him a debt. Beyond that, it seemed that the work was all mine, and I got either the credit or the blame. Most times it felt much more like blame than credit but, either way, I had to work hard and hope that in the end, He'd see fit to forgive me and accept me.

Perhaps you don't see it the same way. If so, I'm glad. But that's what I believed in my heart of hearts.

Since finding out who Jesus is biblically, though, I can only say that my highest praise is owed to Jesus, and this song speaks the joy and devotion that have come to me since knowing a Savior who is truly worthy of praise.

Who Is Jesus?

Blessed assurance, Jesus is mine
O what a foretaste of glory divine!
Heir of salvation, purchase of God,
born of his Spirit, washed in his blood.

Perfect submission, perfect delight,
visions of rapture now burst on my sight;
Angels descending bring from above,
echoes of mercy, whispers of love.

Perfect submission, all is at rest;
I in my Savior am happy and blest,
watching and waiting, looking above,
filled with his goodness, lost in his love.

This is my story, this is my song,
praising my Savior all the day long;
This is my story, this is my song,
praising my Savior all the day long;

(Blessed Assurance, Fanny J. Crosby)

[1]Angels, biblically speaking, are a special creation by God—not men, but not gods,
either. Their job is to serve God and to serve those who believe in God.

". . . and thou shalt know no god but me:
for there is no saviour beside me."
— Hosea 13:4 —

Chapter Eleven

ONE GOD, THREE GODS?

*P*erhaps the single, biggest stumbling block for most of us who have come out of the LDS church is the issue of the trinity. We've spent years learning how that incomprehensible doctrine is at best misguided and, at worst, a product of Satan, and for good reason. Who can imagine a God who's one in three, or three in one, or something crazy like that, all based on a few obscure verses in the book of John.

That sure was my mindset when coming out of the church, and perhaps it's yours now. In fact, for me, this doctrine was such a crazy one that I spent months studying it, just to figure out where Christians were coming from. Before I did that, though, I simply could not understand how intelligent Christians could believe something so incredibly strange.

Before I talk more about how and why I tackled this issue, I want to address God's attributes that seem strange to us. You see, even while LDS, we accepted some concepts about God that were quite difficult to understand. Think for a moment about the idea of God's omnipresence—being able to be everywhere, all the time. That's certainly an attribute that we can't easily conceive, and when we try, we become overwhelmed. Yet, we believe that God is omnipresent.

In addition, the concept of God being omniscient—knowing all things—is something difficult to comprehend because contrary to what our mothers told us, no one we know has, or could have, this ability. The reason we accept these unbelievable aspects about God is because His Word clearly tells us that He has these attributes, even though we can't comprehend them.

Nonetheless, it's not that strange to accept some truths about God that don't make sense to our human, or finite, reasoning. That's because we're talking about an infinite being: a being who is not human in nature and who doesn't have human limitations. You see, God is a being who is above and beyond His creation. He made it and us. He isn't limited by the same limitations that we, His creation, are. He is God, and as God, He's much, much bigger than we imagined Him when we were LDS.

The first thing we need to understand when looking at the doctrine of the trinity is that God—the God of the Bible—is not like us, and we can't put the same limitations on Him that we can put on man. As explained in the chapter about God, that's exactly what He says about Himself in the Bible. "…for I am God, and not man;…" (Hosea 11:9)

The next thing we need to understand about the trinity is just what it is. While I can't speak for you, I can share that when I was LDS, I was subtly influenced that the trinity was some crazy doctrinal teaching that God was one, which ignored the clear scriptural fact that God was three. But that's a misrepresentation of the doctrine of the trinity and simply not true.

One God, Three Gods?

The doctrine of the trinity first and foremost says that God is one, *and also* that God is three. More important, even though I don't understand it any more than I understand God's omniscience or omnipresence, the doctrine of the trinity is man's attempt to understand and explain just what the Bible teaches.

Let me explain. I'm sure you're familiar with scriptures that show that God the Father, God the Son, and God the Holy Spirit are separate spiritual beings, or Gods. The baptism of Jesus (Matthew 3:16-17), the transfiguration of Jesus (Matthew 17:5), or the stoning of Steven (Acts 7:56) are a few examples of where scripture clearly teaches this concept. Yet, the very clear and fundamental teaching of the Bible is that there is one God, and that this God is the ONLY God. Since this is not a clear LDS teaching, let's spend a bit of time looking at what the Bible teaches about this aspect of God.

From the time that Moses led the children of Israel out of Egypt, perhaps the most fundamental difference between Israel and the people around them was their belief in one God. In one of the first commandments that God gave Moses, He said: "Hear, O Israel: The LORD our God is one LORD:" (Deuteronomy 6:4)

Jesus quoted this same verse in Mark 12:29 and called it "the first," or foundation, of all commandments. "And Jesus answered him, 'The first of all the commandments is, Hear, O Israel; The Lord our God is one Lord:'"

Jesus was probably taught this particular scripture from the time he was a young boy in his home, because it was this same passage in Deuteronomy where Moses instructed parents to teach their children this commandment. And if you do a search on the Internet for The Shema, you'll find that it's taught even today to Jewish children as one of their foundational beliefs. It's that important!

Now, if this were the only verse in the Bible that stated God was one, we could say that maybe it doesn't mean that God is ONLY one God, or that the Jewish people had a funny take on who God is, or even just didn't understand that Jesus is the very God, but it's not! Instead, the prophets, under God's divine inspiration throughout the history of Israel, reiterated this particular teaching. Here are a few examples:

> ...I am the first, and I am the last; and beside me there is no God. (Isaiah 44:6)
>
> I am the LORD, and there is none else, there is no God beside me:... (Isaiah 45:5)
>
> ...I am the LORD, and there is none else. (Isaiah 45:6)
>
> ...and thou shalt know no god but me: for there is no saviour beside me. (Hosea 13:4)

These are just a few of the scriptures in the Bible where God says that He is absolutely, positively one God. In fact, in at least twenty-eight verses, God says unequivocally that He is one God.

Before we move on, I want to focus on two more scriptures where God quite clearly says He is one God.

> ...I am he: before me there was no God formed, neither shall there be after me. I, even I, am the LORD; and beside me there is no saviour. (Isaiah 43:10-11)
>
> ...Is there a God beside me? yea, there is no God; I know not any. (Isaiah 44:8)

These two passages clearly teach that God Himself knows of NO other God and that there is no other God or Savior than God Himself. This clearly refutes the LDS teaching that God is one of many gods who had a father god, and a grandfather god and so on, and the LDS teaching that God the Father, Jesus, and the Holy Spirit are three separate Gods.

This aspect is very important to grasp, because one of the hardest concepts about the trinity to comprehend is that it's often nearly impossible in the scriptures to distinguish between God the Father, God the Son, and God the Holy Spirit. In fact, all three have the same attributes: love, mercy, omniscience, omnipresence, eternality, and more.

The next step to understanding the trinity leads us to the biblical teachings about Jesus and the fact that He saw Himself as God, yet with a specific task, His own personality, and His own role in history.

> Therefore the Lord himself shall give you a sign; Behold, a virgin shall conceive, and bear a son, and shall call his name Immanuel. (Isaiah 7:14)
>
> Now all this was done, that it might be fulfilled which was spoken of the Lord by the prophet, saying, "Behold, a virgin shall be with child, and shall bring forth a son, and they shall call his name Emmanuel, which being interpreted is, God with us." (Matthew 1:22-23)

You see, Jesus came to earth to become "God with Us." Another way of saying it is that God Himself became a man and lived among us. Note the titles Isaiah called Jesus while speaking under the inspiration of the Holy Spirit:

> For unto us a child is born, unto us a son is given: and the government shall be upon his shoulder: and his name shall be called Wonderful, Counsellor, The mighty God, The everlasting Father, The Prince of Peace. (Isaiah 9:6)

What's most interesting about these titles is that "Counselor" is the name Jesus gives the Holy Spirit in John 14, and "Everlasting Father" and "Mighty God" are often names used to describe God the Father, yet here they are distinctively given to Jesus.

It's interesting to note in scripture, too, that Jesus claimed to be God. This was one reason that the people were so offended by Him. Remember in the Old Testament when Moses asked God what name he and the Israelites should call Him? God responded with "I Am." (Exodus 3:14) The Hebrew word indicates that God is the self-sufficient one, or the one who needs no one else and nothing else to survive. Note what Jesus said when the people of His day questioned His authority to do what He was doing: "Before Abraham was, I am." (John 8:58)

In this passage, Jesus clearly identified Himself with I AM of the Old Testament. The people of His day knew that this was what Jesus was claiming, because they immediately tried to stone Him for saying this. They knew that what He said, if not true, was blasphemy.

John, too, in his book very clearly tells us that Jesus is God.

> In the beginning was the Word, and the Word was
> with God, and the Word was God…And the Word
> was made flesh, and dwelt among us,… (John 1:1, 14)

Throughout scripture, the Holy Spirit is also referred to equally and in the same manner as God, having the same traits, the same abilities, and being equal to God or one with God. One example is in the story of Ananias. If you recall, in the book of Acts, Ananias sells some property, and then with his wife decides to give part of it while lying to the apostles that he's giving all of it.

> But Peter said, "Ananias, why hath Satan filled thine
> heart to lie to the Holy Ghost, and to keep back part

of the price of the land? Whiles it remained, was it not thine own? and after it was sold, was it not in thine own power? why hast thou conceived this thing in thine heart? thou hast not lied unto men, but unto God." (Acts 5:3-4)

Another passage in Psalms 139 gives the Holy Spirit the same attribute as God, that of omnipresence:

Whither shall I go from thy spirit? or whither shall I flee from thy presence? If I ascend up into heaven, thou art there: if I make my bed in hell, behold, thou art there. (Psalms 139:7-8)

I hope this chapter will help you understand that the doctrine of the trinity is an attempt to explain in a succinct way what the Bible teaches, which is: God is one, and God is three.

As I write this, I struggle with how to explain this concept in more depth. It's huge, I know, and truthfully I can't really wrap my mind around it any more than you can. The one thing I've realized about biblical Christianity is that I have to be willing to accept what the Bible says about absolutely everything without adding more to it and without taking away from it. And that's just what the doctrine of the trinity attempts to do: stay within what the Bible teaches about God and not go beyond it or minimize its truths.

In summary, the Bible teaches that God is:

1. unequivocally one God, and there is no other God. In fact, God Himself clearly states that He knows of, and recognizes, no other God.

2. the One God who makes Himself manifest to us in three personages: God the Father, God the Son (or Jesus), and God the Holy Spirit.

3. all three personages who make up the one God, share the same attributes, and have the same power. They are the same in their power and their abilities but different in the roles they play in our lives and throughout history.

4. God the Father, God the Son, and God the Holy Spirit are fully God and can't be divided out of God.

I started this chapter by sharing with you how I had struggled with this concept, and I mean struggled. I was NOT going to accept this crazy Christian doctrine. But since I had come to see that God wanted us to use His Word to determine truth, I figured I'd better start my arguments by learning what the Bible really had to say first, and determine my doctrine later.

For me, what this meant was that I got out my trusty notebook every time I picked up my Bible, nearly every day, and noted any reference that helped me see better who God, Jesus, and the Holy Spirit claimed to be. After months of doing this, and after I'd read most of the Old Testament and all of the New, I started compiling all my verses into one document.

I then read through what LDS leaders had written about who God was, and later what Christians had written about who God was. I even went as far as to read various theological creeds that lay out the doctrine of the trinity. Finally, after all of that study-ing, I concluded what God actually had to say for Himself. What I found surprised me, as it might you, too. What I found was that the traditional doctrine of the trinity explained just what the Bible taught, and the LDS doctrine did not. To believe LDS doctrine about who God is, you have to ignore, or attempt to explain away, the many scriptures that talk about God being one and His clear statements that no other Gods exist.

I want to reiterate a most critical point for understanding the trinity. The only way to be sure that our doctrine comes from God is to base that doctrine in His Word, the Bible; and the Bible clearly teaches that God is triune in nature.

So, where does that leave you? I suppose in the same place it left me, searching for truth. While you might not be ready to accept this teaching, I plead with you to search out the truth for yourself and to not reject it out-of-hand. The reason that traditional, biblically based Christianity has always believed in the trinitarian doctrine is that it's exactly what God has revealed to us about who He is.

"Therefore being justified by faith,
we have peace with God
through our Lord Jesus Christ:"
— Romans 5:1 —

WHAT DOES GOD WANT
FROM ME?

I've always loved to walk for exercise. When I worked for the City of Phoenix many years ago, I often walked the streets during my lunch hour. One day while walking down the sidewalk, I came across someone who was handing out tracts. Because I believed I was a Christian, although LDS at the time, I thought I'd read one to see what it had to say. So I took the tract and read it. Maybe you've seen the type? It told a nice little story about someone who had been involved in some gross sin, then had turned his life over to Jesus, and Jesus had fixed it. It went on to tell me I had to "get saved," and that I could do so right then and there by praying a simple little prayer. Well, I being one not wanting to leave anything to chance prayed that prayer and…nothing happened. Interesting, I thought, as I threw it in the garbage.

For me, I just didn't understand what that tract had to say. Oftentimes, in the LDS church we use the same terms that Christians use, yet we mean something completely different. That's why I'm trying my best to stay away from using certain terms in this book and, instead, have titled this chapter, "What does God Want from Me?" That's really the crux of the matter. We've seen who God is, we know who we are and that we're in big trouble, so now what does He require of us?

As explained in the chapter, "Who Am I?", we really can't do anything to please God. Remember the verses that state the fact we are sinners both by practice and by birth (Genesis 3 and Romans 3:23), and that sin separates us from a Holy God? Recall from the chapter, "Who is God?", that God is Holy—meaning He's separated from us because of His perfection. We also learned that in Isaiah 64:6, God said we can't do anything by ourselves that'll bring us back into that relationship with Him because all of our so-called righteous acts are in His eyes filthy rags.

"It is a fearful thing to fall into the hands of the living God." (Hebrews 10:31) About now, maybe you can relate to this statement: If God is all that we've read about, it is awe-inspiring, and maybe just a bit scary, to think about approaching Him. So we search for what God wants. For example, ancient peoples gave human sacrifices to appease their gods. The Jewish people, on God's orders, made various burnt offerings to atone for their sins and keep them in His good graces. Today, we also see lots of people doing various things trying to appease, or please, God. We see extremist Muslims hijack airplanes and drive them through buildings, hoping in their sacrifice to obtain eternal reward. And, indeed, the Koran tells them they can achieve it by doing what they did. We see people all over the world giving large portions of their fortunes to TV evangelists hoping to merit a special blessing or healing from God. But is this what God wants from us? If not, what does He want?

What Does God Want?

The simple answer is that God could demand any of those things from us—He has the power and the right. But He didn't. Instead, what God asks of us is a simple act of faith—to believe in Jesus Christ. In exchange for that simple act of faith, God bestows His grace on us with a free gift—the gift of eternal life.

Here are some verses that tell us what God wants from us:

> For God so loved the world, that he gave his only begotten Son, that whosoever believeth in him should not perish, but have everlasting life. (John 3:16)

> For the wages of sin is death; but the gift of God is eternal life through Jesus Christ our Lord. (Romans 6:23)

> For by grace are ye saved through faith; and that not of yourselves: it is the gift of God: Not of works, lest any man should boast. (Ephesians 2:8-9)

In the book of John, John tells us that he wrote his book specifically so we would know how to obtain eternal life. Here's what he said:

> But these are written, that ye might believe that Jesus is the Christ, the Son of God; and that believing ye might have life through his name. (John 20:31)

And it's interesting to note that in the book of John, eighteen times Jesus is quoted as saying, "believe in me." Here are some examples:

> That whosoever *believeth* in him should not perish, but have eternal life. For God so loved the world, that he gave his only begotten Son, that whosoever *believeth* in him should not perish, but have everlasting life. For God sent not his Son into the world to condemn the world; but that the world through him might be saved. He that *believeth* on him is not condemned: but

he that *believeth* not is condemned already, because he hath not *believed* in the name of the only begotten Son of God. (John 3:15-18)

Verily, verily, I say unto you, He that heareth my word, and *believeth* on him that sent me, hath everlasting life, and shall not come into condemnation; but is passed from death unto life. (John 5:24)

Jesus answered and said unto them, "This is the work of God, that ye *believe* on him whom he hath sent." (John 6:29)

I could go on and on, up to eighteen times! Instead, I highly suggest you read the book of John for yourself. Keep in mind just what John wrote about and why—that you might see that Jesus is the promised Messiah, and that you might believe in Him and have eternal life.

At this point you might be thinking, *What about James 2?* I'll get to James 2 in another chapter. For now, I want to address in detail the more important question of what God wants from us.

The simple fact is what God wants from us first and foremost is to believe in Him, and in Jesus, and in the finished work of Jesus on the cross. God wants us to believe the fact that Jesus fully paid our sin debt—for all sin—those we've already committed, those we're committing, and those we will commit.

The book of Romans explains this issue in detail and answers various questions we might ask. In Romans 4, we read:

What shall we say then that Abraham our father, as pertaining to the flesh, hath found? For if Abraham were justified by works, he hath whereof to glory; but not before God. For what saith the scripture?

> Abraham believed God, and it was counted unto him
> for righteousness. (Romans 4:1-3)

First, Paul begins this chapter talking about Abraham—someone the Jewish people greatly respected. He takes us back to the story when God first met and talked with Abraham and promised him a son. (Genesis 15) Did you know that it was fifteen years later, and after Ishmael was born, that God finally "made good" on that promise? And did you realize that several more years went by before God asked Abraham to sacrifice Isaac, and Abraham obeyed God? This is an interesting point to note, especially in light of what James teaches in James 2, and we'll get to that. But first look at what the very next sentence says:

> Now to him that worketh is the reward not reckoned
> of grace, but of debt. But to him that worketh not,
> but believeth on him that justifieth the ungodly, his
> faith is counted for righteousness. (Romans 4:4-5)

It's really a simple concept. When we work for someone, we deserve the pay for the work we've done. We see it every week, or biweekly, with our paychecks. We'd never, ever call our paycheck grace. We might think it was an act of grace to have a job, but we know that we've earned our paychecks. Well, it's the same in scripture. We either do good works to try to pay for our sins and get the wages for all our hard work, or we let Jesus pay for them. Remember we learned before that if we choose to try to pay for our own sins, we're lost because all of our works are of no value to God, but instead are like filthy rags. (Isaiah 64:6)

The next eleven verses (Romans 4:5-15) talk about why that grace could be given to us. The bottom line is that the promise to Abraham, that through his seed would come salvation, wasn't meant for only circumcised Jewish people but also for those who are spiritually Abraham's children. We become Abraham's children by placing our faith in Jesus Christ. Verse 16 sums it up by saying that it had to be an act of grace from God—meaning that we couldn't do anything to earn our salvation.

> Therefore it is of faith, that it might be by grace; to the end the promise might be sure to all the seed; not to that only which is of the law, but to that also which is of the faith of Abraham; who is the father of us all, (As it is written, "I have made thee a father of many nations,") before him whom he believed, even God, who quickeneth the dead, and calleth those things which be not as though they were. (Romans 4:16-17)

Then the next five verses, I believe, are the *absolute best* definition of saving faith I've found in the Bible:

> Who against hope believed in hope, that he might become the father of many nations, according to that which was spoken, So shall thy seed be. And being not weak in faith, he considered not his own body now dead, when he was about an hundred years old, neither yet the deadness of Sarah's womb: He staggered not at the promise of God through unbelief; but was strong in faith, giving glory to God; And being fully persuaded that, what he had promised, he was able also to perform. And therefore it was imputed to him for righteousness. (Romans 4:18-22)

Think about it for a moment. Nothing Abraham or Sarah could do could make an heir—nothing. Abraham was about 100 years old and, yes, I'll acknowledge that men can still produce children at that age. Sarah was also old, and scripture says that her womb was dead or, in other words, she'd gone through menopause already. Yet Abraham ignored all of that and decided to believe God. He took God's word at face value and was fully persuaded that what God had promised, He was able to perform.

Scripture says Abraham even gave glory to God and that it was imputed to him for righteousness. Impute is a word meaning credited to, and it's used in the same way we'd use it when we go to the bank to deposit money. We would give the money to the clerk and they would credit it to, or impute it to, our account. In the same way, God credited Abraham with Jesus' righteousness when he believed.

And that's just what God does for us. When we put our faith in Jesus Christ, we are then imputed with His righteousness.

If we go back to the scale picture displayed in the chapter, "Who Am I?", the good end of our scale just went flying through the air as Jesus' perfect righteousness increases on our side while our efforts disappear.

Romans 5 continues the theme by saying:

> Therefore being justified by faith, we have peace with God through our Lord Jesus Christ: By whom also we have access by faith into this grace wherein we stand, and rejoice in hope of the glory of God. (Romans 5:1-2)

Justified is another word with a real big meaning. One source defines it as: "God's act of declaring or making a sinner righteous before God." That's just what happens—we're made right before God by faith. Before we leave this theme and go on to some common LDS objections, I want to point out just a few more verses in Romans 5. These are some of my favorite verses in the whole Bible because they truly show God's amazing love for us:

> For when we were yet without strength, in due time Christ died for the ungodly. For scarcely for a righteous man will one die: yet peradventure for a good man some would even dare to die. But God commendeth his love toward us, in that, while we were yet sinners, Christ died for us. Much more then, being now justified by his blood, we shall be saved from wrath through him. For if, when we were enemies, we were reconciled to God by the death of his Son, much more, being reconciled, we shall be saved by his life. (Romans 5:6-10)

What I want to point out are the terms God uses to describe us in this passage: ungodly (verse 6), sinners (verse 8), and enemies (verse 10). Paul isn't talking about someone who's a repentant sinner that God chose to forgive, but rather a blatant and ungodly sinner, his enemy. Wow! Now that's powerful. Think back to what we've learned about ourselves in previous chapters, and that's just who we are—ungodly sinners and enemies of God.

Knowing this, what then does God want from us? He wants us to trust that He can do just what He said He would—take ungodly sinners and enemies, and make them into His own dear children by His grace. It's that simple.

What about those objections we all have? Would it surprise you to know that Paul addresses those too? "What shall we say then? Shall we continue in sin, that grace may abound?" (Romans 6:1)

Paul's resounding answer is ABSOLUTELY NOT (or God forbid in the King James Version). Paul explains that the reason we don't continue in sin isn't that we're trying to please God, because we've already learned that we can't do that. Instead, God does a work in us, changing us into a new people, those who don't have the same desires as they did before and who don't look at things the same way anymore.

You see, when you place your faith in Jesus Christ, things happen—radical things, amazing things, things that only the Holy Spirit working within you can cause to happen. Some people, for example, are instantly cured of sin problems they've struggled with for quite some time—such as alcoholism, using bad language, smoking, and more. Most people find that they develop a new love for the Bible. Many say that they see things clearly for the first time, even though they might have read the Bible before. For me, I developed a passion for prayer, so much so that whenever I had a quiet moment by myself, I'd find myself praying.

There are many, many things that happen to people when they truly put their faith in Jesus. And, biblically speaking, they all make sense. Here are some of the transformations the Bible emphasizes:

> Therefore if any man be in Christ, he is a new creature: old things are passed away; behold, all things are become new. (2 Corinthians 5:17)
>
> ...that we might receive the adoption of sons. And because ye are sons, God hath sent forth the Spirit of his Son into your hearts, crying, "Abba, Father." (Galatians 4:4-6)
>
> In whom also we have obtained an inheritance, (Ephesians 1:11)
>
> In whom ye also trusted, after that ye heard the word of truth, the gospel of your salvation: in whom also after that ye believed, ye were sealed with that holy Spirit of promise, Which is the earnest of our inheritance until the redemption of the purchased possession, unto the praise of his glory. (Ephesians 1:13-14)

> And we are his witnesses of these things; and so is
> also the Holy Ghost, whom God hath given to them
> that obey him. (Acts 5:32)

When we put our faith in Jesus Christ, we can expect much, much more. The bottom line, however, is that we become a new people. We are no longer a people "dead in trespasses and sins," and "children of wrath" as described in Ephesians 2:1,3. Instead, we become alive to Christ, and God sees us as being "in Christ." Because we are new people having the Holy Spirit within us, we have new thoughts, new desires, and new life—really. And in this new life we do good things—things that truly are good in God's eyes, things that please Him.

Earlier, I mentioned Ephesians 2:8-9 regarding the fact that we are saved only by putting our faith in Jesus Christ and not by doing any works. Now let's look at Ephesians 2:10, the very next verse:

> For we are his workmanship, created in Christ Jesus
> unto good works, which God hath before ordained
> that we should walk in them. (Ephesians 2:10)

You see, Christians are saved through Jesus' righteousness and recreated by the Holy Spirit to do good works, and so we should do good things.

Our focus, though, in doing these good works is different than it was when we were LDS and did good works. That's because our focus now is on being in a living, breathing relationship with God, where everything we do flows from Him and the relationship we share with Him. In other words, our focus is on God Himself rather than on what we should or should not do That's because the most important thing that happens in salvation is that we are restored to a place of fellowship with God. We once again have a relationship with Him and can give Him glory by walking with Him, much like Adam did in the Garden of Eden. You'll read more about this in the next chapter, "What Do I Do Now?" For now, know that God desires to have fellowship with you—that's what His plan has been from the beginning. It's why He walked with Adam and Eve in the garden, and why we yearn deep down in our souls for that fellowship once more. Some say that we have a God-sized hole in our hearts. I think that's a good description. Nothing but God can ever fill that hole. There is no way we can fill that hole but to do it God's way, which is to put our faith in Jesus Christ for our salvation.

"Abide in me, and I in you.
As the branch cannot bear fruit of itself,
except it abide in the vine…."
—John 15:4 —

Chapter Thirteen

WHAT DO I DO NOW?

This morning while writing, I've also done a variety of other tasks. I've washed two loads of clothes, folded them, and put them away. I've washed some dishes, dusted some furniture, thought about what to cook for dinner, and straightened up the house. I do these chores, not because I love them, but because I'm a mom and, honestly, they're what most moms do. I realize your mom might not have done all of these, but I think we could agree that doing household chores are generally what we'd consider normal for moms.

Similarly, as Christians, we do good works because that's who God made us. But, there's much more. It's not just about us and what we do, rather it's about a relationship—a very special relationship—one with the King of the Universe. And we obtain this relationship by believing God will be faithful to do what He says He will do. That's what putting our faith in Jesus is all about.

As we go along in that relationship, we find that we maintain it by faith, as well.

> As ye have therefore received Christ Jesus the Lord,
> so *walk ye in him:* Rooted and built up in him, and sta-
> blished in the faith, as ye have been taught, abound-
> ing therein with thanksgiving. (Colossians 2:6-7)

So how do we go about maintaining this faith relationship? Well, the first and perhaps the most important thing we can do, is to make some time each and every day to spend with Him. The Bible calls those who are believers the "bride" of Christ, and in many ways that's a good analogy. Just as you wouldn't expect to build a good relationship with your spouse without spending time with him or her, you can't have a very good relationship with God without spending time with Him.

During this time that you spend with Him, talk with Him. Tell Him your deepest longings, your fears, your hurts, and your dreams. Then listen as He responds. Probably the most common way He'll respond to you is through His written Word. Remember what II Timothy 3 says about God's Word? It says that God's Word gives us reproof, correction, and instructions in righteousness, as well as doctrine. Therefore, it's natural that God would regularly use His Word to show us who He is and what He wants. That's why it's important to spend some time reading from His Word, too.

Another thing that will be very helpful in your Christian life is to attend a good, solid, Bible-teaching church.

> And he gave some, apostles; and some, prophets; and
> some, evangelists; and some, pastors and teachers; For
> the perfecting of the saints, for the work of the minis-
> try, for the edifying of the body of Christ: Till we all
> come in the unity of the faith, and of the knowledge
> of the Son of God, unto a perfect man, unto the

measure of the stature of the fulness of Christ: That we henceforth be no more children, tossed to and fro, and carried about with every wind of doctrine, by the sleight of men, and cunning craftiness, whereby they lie in wait to deceive; But speaking the truth in love, may grow up into him in all things, which is the head, even Christ: (Ephesians 4:11-15)

It's part of God's design that He gives to all of us different gifts—different abilities with which we can grow and help each other grow in the body of Christ—the church. It's important that we are a part of that body, allowing our gifts to grow within that body, and being edified by other people's gifts. Assembling together as part of a body is so important that the book of Hebrews specifically instructs Christians to meet together with other believers:

Not forsaking the assembling of ourselves together, as the manner of some is; but exhorting one another: and so much the more, as ye see the day approaching. (Hebrews 10:25)

When we meet together with other believers, we learn from them, we encourage them, and we grow in our Christian walk in ways that we just couldn't grow if we stayed away. Remember that meeting together with others who also believe in Christ is what church is in its most basic form.

Keep in mind, also, that your relationship with Jesus is a walk—a journey rather than a destination. And, it's a journey you'll learn about as you spend time in His Word, in prayer, in church, and by daily living your Christian life. In John 15, Jesus gives my favorite description of the Christian life.

Abide in me, and I in you. As the branch cannot bear fruit of itself, except it abide in the vine; no more can ye, except ye abide in me. I am the vine, ye are the branches: He that abideth in me, and I in him, the same bringeth forth much fruit: for without me ye can do nothing. (John 15:4-5)

A very graphic illustration of this truth happened to a friend of mine who once had a very beautiful flowering vine growing along her back fence. In the spring, the flowers would cover the back wall of her garden, creating a beautiful fragrance and delighting everyone who saw it. One winter, however, when she was weeding her garden, she snipped the wrong branch and disconnected half of the vine. She didn't notice it at the time, but a few weeks later, that half of the vine had withered and died. Ultimately, she had to pull it out and throw it away. It simply couldn't live while disconnected from the root. That's the same illustration Jesus gives us for living the Christian life. We've got to have that connection to Him or we'll wither and die, and we've got to have that connection to produce fruit in our lives. Just as my friend's vine could no longer produce beautiful flowers once she disconnected it from the vine, we cannot produce fruit in our lives when we're not living in an active relationship with Jesus.

In fact, scripture says that when we try to produce fruit using our own strength and power, we do it apart from the vine. As a result, any seeming fruit we produce would be weak, ineffective, or just plain rotten. That type of fruit doesn't spring from the true vine, Jesus, but instead springs from human efforts. The simple fact is that we've got to be connected to the vine, which is Jesus, or we'll die. Good habits such as spending time with Jesus in prayer, reading His Word, and going to church are just that— habits that help us maintain the relationship that is the lifeblood of the Christian life.

Oh, and one more thing. You're going to sin. Does that shock you? It shouldn't. You see, God does many wonderful things inside of us when we become Christians, yet He doesn't completely take away our human, or sinful, nature. So at times, we will sin, make bad choices, and walk in the flesh instead of in the Spirit. Paul talks about this issue in Romans 7, and says:

> We know that the law is spiritual; but I am unspiritual, sold as a slave to sin. I do not understand what I do. For what I want to do I do not do, but what I hate I do. And if I do what I do not want to do, I agree that the law is good. As it is, it is no longer I myself who do it, but it is sin living in me. I know that nothing good lives in me, that is, in my sinful nature. For I have the desire to do what is good, but I cannot carry it out. For what I do is not the good I want to do; no, the evil I do not want to do—this I keep on doing. Now if I do what I do not want to do, it is no longer I who do it, but it is sin living in me that does it. So I find this law at work: When I want to do good, evil is right there with me. For in my inner being I delight in God's law; but I see another law at work in the members of my body, waging war against the law of my mind and making me a prisoner of the law of sin at work within my members. What a wretched man I am! Who will rescue me from this body of death? (Romans 7:14-24 NIV)

As we can see, this struggle against sin was a great burden for Paul. Paul wanted to serve God with all his heart, yet he found himself failing as he gave in to what his "flesh" wanted. And every Christian who has ever lived, if they're honest, would say they have the same battle. We want to do the right thing, but we fail. I know that I've had mornings where I'd woke up early, had a wonderful time with the Lord, read the Bible, talked to Him, heard from Him, and more, and then after I'd sent my kids off to school, had a big argument with my husband—ugh!

In Romans 8, Paul gives us the answer to this dilemma. It is to simply "walk in the Spirit." Galatians 5 tells us to walk in the Spirit and we will not fulfill the lusts of the flesh, and that's so true. As Christians, we have the choice to "walk in the flesh," which means that we do what we think is right, go after those things we want, follow ways we think are good, and more. We also have the choice to "walk in the Spirit" and do those things that God thinks are right, pursue those things God wants, and follow after those things God says are good.

Know that walking in the Spirit is a progressive learning experience. We won't understand it perfectly when we're new Christians, and we'll probably mess up later on too! But God knew that also and gave us a solution:

> If we confess our sins, he is faithful and just to forgive
> us our sins, and to cleanse us from all unrighteousness.
> (1 John 1:9)

That's right, when we mess up, God simply expects us to confess that sin to Him, and it's gone, just like that. We're as fresh and clean as any newborn Christian all over again. Of course, if our sin is one that needs some restitution, we should do that. The good thing is we don't really have to worry about what we should do, because God will talk to us in each and every situation, either through His Word, or by simply knowing He's saying something to us through His Holy Spirit within us. He will lead and guide us as to what we should do. That's what the Christian walk is all about after all—a living, breathing relationship between us and the living God.

A friend of mine had to go to Cuba for a ministry assignment for a month. After he left, I connected with his wife on Facebook. It was both cute and heartwarming to see her anguish over her husband not being home. Every day she'd comment such as, "day 4 of 27, I sure miss my husband" and "I think it is a good thing my husband will be home soon." All of us who watched her drama were touched by her true and tender love for her husband even after they had been married quite awhile; they have a daughter who's in her twenties. One day it was a bit of a shock, however, to see her response to someone in which she wrote, "It took wading through some really tough years and getting some great counseling, but we are now in an amazing and wonderful place. I highly recommend toughing out the crappy years. I also recommend good marriage counseling. It makes the great years all the sweeter."

Your relationship with God biblically can be compared to a marriage relationship. You're going to have some times when God seems so real, so vivid, so "there" that you'll be blown away. You'll also have times that will be more of a struggle, when it will seem as though your prayers are just bouncing off the ceiling, when life will be so hard that you won't be sure God cares. The difference between my friend's marriage and your relationship with God is this: God is perfect, unlike my friend. And because He's perfect, everything He'll do for you will be for your own good, even when you might not see that goodness. Your relationship with God will also be like the relationship my friend has with his wife—a relationship full of love, full of compassion, and painful when you're apart. This is the relationship God wants to have with you, one where twenty-plus years from now you'll still be blown away by who He is and by what He's done in your life.

And that's just what the Christian life is all about—living in that relationship with Him. It's not about following a bunch of rules—although you will be doing just that. Instead, your focus will be on the Creator of the rules—the loving, all-caring, and compassionate Creator who wants nothing more than to enjoy His time with you forever.

Chapter Fourteen

WHAT ABOUT JAMES 2?

What doth it profit, my brethren, though a man say he hath faith, and have not works? can faith save him? . . . Even so faith, if it hath not works, is dead, being alone. (James 2:14, 17)

If you're a typical LDS person or an ex-LDS person, about now you're thinking, *But what about James 2?* You're absolutely right! James 2 is part of God's inspired Word, so we can't ignore what it says—even when it seems to contradict what the rest of the Bible says. The clue to understanding James 2 lies in a fact. That fact is that God will not contradict Himself. That means that we have to look at James 2 in light of all the other verses we've already learned about that seem to say very clearly that we cannot work for our salvation.

So what is James talking about? Well, the rest of the passage helps us understand just what James is talking about. Let's look at it here:

What doth it profit, my brethren, though a man say he hath faith, and have not works? can faith save him? If a brother or sister be naked, and destitute of daily food, And one of you say unto them, Depart in peace, be ye warmed and filled; notwithstanding ye give them not those things which are needful to the body; what doth it profit? Even so faith, if it hath not works, is dead, being alone. Yea, a man may say, Thou hast faith, and I have works: shew me thy faith without thy works, and I will shew thee my faith by my works. Thou believest that there is one God; thou doest well: the devils also believe, and tremble. But wilt thou know, O vain man, that faith without works is dead? Was not Abraham our father justified by works, when he had offered Isaac his son upon the altar? Seest thou how faith wrought with his works, and by works was faith made perfect? And the scripture was fulfilled which saith, Abraham believed God, and it was imputed unto him for righteousness: and he was called the Friend of God. Ye see then how that by works a man is justified, and not by faith only. Likewise also was not Rahab the harlot justified by works, when she had received the messengers, and had sent them out another way? For as the body without the spirit is dead, so faith without works is dead also. (James 2: 14-26)

I believe the key to understanding James is in the two examples he gives: the first being about Abraham offering Isaac on the altar, and the second being about Rahab, the harlot. You're probably familiar with the story of Isaac and Abraham, and how

God told Abraham to sacrifice his son, Isaac. Abraham obeyed and packed up his son, some wood, and went to the mountain to sacrifice Isaac. When Abraham was just ready to do it, God stilled his hand, and instead provided a ram for the sacrifice.

You may not be as familiar with the story of Rahab. It occurs in Joshua 2 and tells about when Joshua sent two spies into Jericho to spy on the city. They met Rahab there, and she told them she believed they were going to win the battle. Then, instead of turning them in, Rahab agreed to hide them and lead the men from her city astray when they came looking for them to kill them.

Before I explain why I think the key to understanding this passage is in these examples, let's go back and see how this particular passage starts: "What doth it profit, my brethren...." (James 2:14)

Immediately preceding this passage are verses that talk about how we live out our faith, specifically how we should act when a rich man and a poor man come into our church. That's the theme that James continues with when he says, "What does it profit us...." He's talking about the practical outworking of our faith—how we act as Christians.

I'm sure you've heard horror stories about Christians doing all kinds of terrible things and calling themselves Christians—honestly, they gave us all black eyes! My personal experience included a woman who said, "Praise Jesus," every time she turned around, and then asked me to lie for her while she cheated on her husband. This is exactly what James is talking about—how we live our Christian lives. He's telling us that if we don't walk the walk, our faith is, in essence, dead—not that we're not saved, but instead our faith is a dead faith. It's lifeless, and worthless, and well, just useless.

Other verses assure us that if we've put our faith in Jesus Christ, we are saved.

Now let's go back to the examples that James gives:

> Was not Abraham our father justified by works, when he had offered Isaac his son upon the altar? Seest thou how faith wrought with his works, and by works was faith made perfect? And the scripture was fulfilled which saith, Abraham believed God, and it was imputed unto him for righteousness: and he was called the Friend of God. Ye see then how that by works a man is justified, and not by faith only.
> (James 2:21-24)

Abraham's dealings with God started in Genesis 12. Scripture says that Abraham was seventy-five-years-old when God told him to leave Haran and head to the land that God had promised him. It was then that Abraham built his first altar and called on the name of the Lord—in other words, Abraham believed God right then and there. Of course, Abraham did a bit of wandering, went into Egypt, came out of Egypt, went to the Negev and to Bethel, and finally settled in the land of Caanan. Finally, in Genesis 15, God promises Abraham he'll have a son. Scripture records that Abraham believed God then. "Abram believed the LORD, and he credited it to him as righteousness." (Genesis 15:6 NIV)

What's interesting about that statement is that Paul quoted it in both Romans 4 and Galatians 3 when he was using Abraham as an example to prove that God saves people without works. Let's look at those verses so we can see how Paul used them:

> What shall we say then that Abraham our father, as pertaining to the flesh, hath found? For if Abraham

were justified by works, he hath whereof to glory; but not before God. For what saith the scripture? Abraham believed God, and it was counted unto him for righteousness. Now to him that worketh is the reward not reckoned of grace, but of debt. But to him that worketh not, but believeth on him that justifieth the ungodly, his faith is counted for righteousness. (Romans 4:1-5)

Are ye so foolish? having begun in the Spirit, are ye now made perfect by the flesh? Have ye suffered so many things in vain? if it be yet in vain. He therefore that ministereth to you the Spirit, and worketh miracles among you, doeth he it by the works of the law, or by the hearing of faith? Even as Abraham believed God, and it was accounted to him for righteousness. (Galatians 3:3-6)

Years went by, and since Sarah hadn't become pregnant, she thought she'd found the solution to God's problem by providing Hagar as a concubine to Abraham. Abraham was eighty-six when Ishmael was born, but Ishmael wasn't God's plan for Abraham. Eventually, when Abraham was one-hundred-years-old, God gave him the son He'd promised through Sarah, his wife. This promise was fulfilled about twenty-five years after God first started dealing with Abraham. Then the scriptures go on to reveal that, "some time later," Abraham was called by God to sacrifice his son.

The reason I went through this chronology is that it's important to note that Abraham had put his faith in God many years before he was called to sacrifice Isaac. And James knew this as well.

When James wrote that Abraham was "justified" by works, it seems clear that he couldn't have been talking about being justified in the same sense we talk about it when we're saved. Here's where I believe the examples help us see just what James was saying. He wrote that Abraham was justified before the world, in his witness to the world, when he was called to sacrifice Isaac. That's just what we do when we treat the poor man right who walks into our church. We're justified, not before God because He knows where we are spiritually—there's no faking it with Him—but instead, we're justified as Christians. The world can see that we're Christians because of what we do.

The story of Rahab carries the same idea. Rahab had heard about the children of Israel—indeed all of Jericho had heard about what God was doing when Israel crossed the Jordan on dry land and defeated their enemies within clear view of Jericho. The difference, though, was that Rahab chose to believe that this God was a God she could believe in—the rest of Jericho did not. So, in a very real sense, Rahab also had put her faith in God before the world saw her acting it out. But when she choose to hide the spies and later hang a red flag in her window, she was acting out her faith for all to see. She was showing that her faith was an active faith—a living faith and a real faith—when she "did" what she believed.

The same is true for us. Our faith is truly a dead faith if we say we've put our faith in Jesus and choose to live in a way that's contrary to that faith.

Now, to compare James 2 with what we've read in other scriptures, let's go back to Ephesians.

> For by grace are ye saved through faith; and that not
> of yourselves: it is the gift of God: Not of works, lest

any man should boast. For we are his workmanship, created in Christ Jesus unto good works, which God hath before ordained that we should walk in them. (Ephesians 2:8-10)

Our salvation, or our justification, of being made right and reconciled with God, and being changed into a new person, resulting in the indwelling of the Holy Spirit, is something we can't do—ever. Jesus had to do it. Our only options are to believe or not to believe. Once we have received this free gift, however, we must act on it as well. But our work is not like the work we did before—a chore or something we have to do to please God. Instead, it is a conscious outworking of what God is doing in us. During that process, the world sees that we are Christians and that God is truly working in us. That's living faith! It's an active living, breathing relationship with God where He's working out what He wants within us, and we're stepping out in faith and doing it.

I suppose, in some respects, it's the difference between when we "command" our children to do a chore and they do it begrudgingly, and when they do it because they want to without us even asking them to do it. For example, we might even have to threaten, cajole, bribe, and more to get our children to do what we ask. That's what we did before for God. We did things for God because we thought we could get something from Him—His goodwill, most likely, but also maybe a very direct blessing—like in the promises of Malachi 2.

Biblical obedience and faith are more like when our children decide they want to help because they love us. Suddenly we can't get them to stop helping. They'll clean their rooms, do an amazing job and even spend hours doing it. We can hardly believe they are the same children we had to threaten before. The difference is that they do it all because they want to.

As you walk in a relationship with the Lord, He puts the desire in your heart to serve Him. By keeping in His Word and seeking His will, you'll find that you desire to please Him and will live out your faith willingly and actively. And, over time, you'll see that you're blessed for doing the things He wants—maybe not in the way you'd thought you might be blessed, but instead through having a more open and closer relationship with Him. And as you grow in that relationship, you'll desire that closeness more and more. You'll find that, like Abraham, you are willing to do anything the Lord asks you to do. And you know what? The world will see and know that you're a Christian. Like with Rahab in Jericho, the world will have no doubt where your loyalties lie.

There's a saying going around that says this: "If you were arrested for being a Christian, would there be enough evidence to convict you?" That's just what James is saying. If there's not enough evidence to convict you of being a Christian, your faith is dead. Not that you haven't put your faith in Jesus for salvation—you may well have. And if you haven't, you should! Instead, if you're not "doing" the things God directs you to do, you're missing out on a living, breathing relationship with the Living God. You're missing out in the one thing in life that will give you true joy, happiness, and peace. And the world, your friends, family, and acquaintances won't be fooled either!

In answer to the question, "What about James 2?" The answer is—absolutely! James 2 is an important part of our Christian walk and life. We should live out our faith and not have a dead faith. It's important—vital even to the Christian life. And, most importantly, it fits in perfectly with what the rest of the Bible teaches about salvation—that it is by faith alone, by the grace of the Lord Jesus Christ. That too is a vital faith, a living faith, one in which we Christians live out what our Master is directing in our lives. It's a faith that brings peace and joy beyond our imagination.

"Let us therefore follow after the things which make for peace and things wherewith we may edify another."

— Romans 14:19 —

Chapter Fifteen

THE SABBATH,
THE WORD OF WISDOM,
AND OTHER BITS OF LEGALISM

an I confess to you that for the first couple of years out of the LDS church I was very judgmental? I believed, like most good LDS people, that I knew what the biblical laws were and that everyone else should live their Christian life like I lived mine. On a practical side, what that meant was that when my coworker and her son participated in a sports tournament on Sunday, I believed they were evil Sabbath breakers. In addition, when others I knew went to a restaurant on Sunday after church, they were causing someone else to sin by working on Sunday and, therefore, were guilty before God of that person's sin. Also, when my husband, who had developed a taste for coffee, made coffee in our house, I allowed it but under the surface was seething about how nasty a habit it really was.

One day, on my way home from church, as I was ranting and raving about "those" Christians who broke the Sabbath, my husband suggested something profound. He suggested to me that I research why those Christians didn't keep the Sabbath, instead of assuming they were sinning. I did the research, and what I found out was very interesting.

Before I explain to you what I found, let's talk about the issue of legalism. It's a term we hear bandied about in Christianity, yet sometimes it's hard to pinpoint just what it means. The Pharisees in the Bible were legalists. What that means is that their allegiance, in a sense, was to the law. In some ways, this seems to have been a good thing, but the trouble was that the Pharisees, in their devotion to the law, had missed knowing Jesus. That's just what happens to us when we slavishly follow the law but don't do what is necessary to know Jesus. It is, in many ways, what happens naturally and is much, much easier than taking the time and energy to come to know God and be in a relationship with Him. Truthfully, it's the kind of life we were taught to live while LDS—to follow the laws for the law's sake and to not spend much time and effort developing a relationship with Jesus.

It's important, first, for us to understand that legalism is not a good thing in a Christian's life, even though we should live the commandments. Instead, what is important in a Christian's life is that we maintain a living, breathing relationship with Jesus. As a result, everything we do will stem from this relationship and not from keeping dry, dead laws.

On the issue of the Sabbath, well, after researching it, this is what I learned. Many Christians believe the Sabbath, as we see it kept by the Jewish people, really doesn't pertain to modern-day Christianity. They believe this for the following biblical reasons.

First, the law to keep the Sabbath was a sign between God and His chosen people, Israel. As such, it could pertain to the Church today or it could not. What I mean is that when Jesus came, He did away with, or completed, the laws that the Jewish people kept. While some may argue against this, very few Christians, for example, keep all 600+ Jewish laws that were kept back then, and I don't know of any Christians who would do the animal sacrifices that were done in Old Testament times. Remember, the animal sacrifices specifically were symbolic of Christ's coming, so to keep them would be to forget or deny that Jesus did what He did.

However, as we know, we do keep some of the Jewish laws like "Thou shalt not kill" or "Thou shalt not commit adultery." What most Christians do to determine which ones to keep in this time is go to the New Testament and find out what "laws" are reiterated, or commanded, in the New Testament.

To finish working through the issue of the Sabbath, let me explain what many Christians think about it. Throughout the Gospels, Jesus reiterates many of the Jewish laws. He tells the rich young ruler, for example, that: "Thou shalt do no murder, Thou shalt not commit adultery, Thou shalt not steal, Thou shalt not bear false witness." Interestingly, He reiterates only nine of the Ten Commandments, but He never, ever mentions keeping the Sabbath. Indeed, many of the Old Testament laws are reiterated in the New Testament but never the command to obey the Sabbath. Many Christians believe this was because Sabbath keeping was a commandment between the nation of Israel and God that was supposed to be a sign of their devotion to Him, and that it was never intended as a sign for us, the Church. Further, in the New Testament we see many things we are to do to show our devotion to God, but Sabbath keeping is never mentioned.

The book of Hebrews, however, talks a lot about a Sabbath rest. Remember, that in the beginning, God rested on the seventh day? Hebrews teaches that Christians have entered into the Sabbath day rest because of Jesus. To further explain, this means our Sabbath day really is not one day in seven, but instead is every day. We live in the Sabbath—in other words, we "rest" in what Jesus has already done.

To the contrary, some Christians do keep the Sabbath. They argue that the Ten Commandments, which they call the moral law, were not completed or done away with in Jesus. Therefore, they believe they are just as responsible to live every point of it now as they were in Jewish days, which of course leads the Christian to Christ since they can't live that moral law and need a Savior. So we can see that this group of Christians bases their belief about the Sabbath on what the Bible teaches, just as clearly as the other group.

Here's where it's so important for us to understand that our relationship with Jesus Christ is just that—our relationship. And because it's our relationship, we might have some strong feelings, commonly called convictions, about some things. Yet, another, just as devoted Christian, might have no convictions over that same issue whatsoever. Keep in mind, scripture directs that we must follow our convictions, and our Christian brothers and sisters must follow theirs. To not do so would be sin, in fact. "…for whatsoever is not of faith is sin." (Romans 14:23)

In a previous chapter, I mentioned the axiom, "In Essentials, Unity; in Non-essentials, Liberty; in All Things, Charity." This principle, while not straight from the Bible, is actually based on biblical teachings. Romans 14 and 15, for instance, go to great lengths to talk about how we Christians can give one another liberty to have different, but equally, biblically based opinions.

> Who art thou that judgest another man's servant? to
> his own master he standeth or falleth. Yea, he shall

be holden up: for God is able to make him stand. (Romans 14:4)

Remember, our Christian life is all about our personal relationship with the Lord. The same is true for every Christian. They, too, are responsible to work out with God exactly what their Christian life should look like in those areas where the Bible is not absolutely clear. This distinction is important to note, because the Bible is absolutely clear on certain issues: infidelity is one; lying is another.

The opposite of living in a living, breathing relationship with God is called legalism. And legalism is how we lived when we were LDS. Legalism isn't only following the rules, but also focusing our attention on the rules to the extent the rule and following the rule becomes more important than our relationship with Jesus.

Honestly, that's what I was doing when I was focusing on the Sabbath day. I saw a rule in the Bible—a valid rule— a rule that I was sure was God's will for all. I was focusing on that rule instead of living in a relationship with God where I asked Him for guidance on how to follow this rule and, just as important, allow others the freedom to follow this "rule" as they, in their relationships with Him, saw fit.

The Word of Wisdom is another issue that we, as LDS people, were quite legalistic about. Would it surprise you to know that the Bible never addresses coffee or tea? And, that the Bible, when addressing alcohol, only addresses as sin those who drink to drunkenness? The Bible does talk about not being addicted or enslaved to anything other than the Lord. That scripture could be construed to mean that we should not drink alcohol or use tobacco, and that we should be very careful about other things that could addict us.

Again, there is no clear list of dos and don'ts in the Bible about the issues the Word of Wisdom covers.

Honestly, we can become so fixated about so many issues affecting the Christian life and, worse, we can judge others over them. Think for a moment about the books we read, the kind of music we listen to, the movies we watch, the food we eat or don't eat, the holidays we celebrate or don't celebrate, how we worship, how we pray, and much, much more. And, since we often have strong opinions about these issues, we can become very judgmental about them.

> Let us not therefore judge one another any more: but judge this rather, that no man put a stumbling block or an occasion to fall in his brother's way. (Romans 14:13)
> Therefore judge nothing before the time, until the Lord come, who both will bring to light the hidden things of darkness, and will make manifest the counsels of the hearts: and then shall every man have praise of God. (1 Corinthians 4:5)
> Let no man therefore judge you in meat, or in drink, or in respect of an holy day, or of the new moon, or of the sabbath days: (Colossians 2:16)

One of the hardest things about leaving Mormonism was not having all these things spelled out. I don't know about you, but I even had my Stake President advising me on what movies to watch, and what movies not to watch. For example, R rated movies were out, just about everything else was in. The problem was, I truly didn't learn how to judge for myself. Honestly, I missed some good movies because they were rated R, although few I admit, and I watched some really trashy ones because they weren't rated R.

As a Christian, I know now that it's my responsibility to go to God with all of these issues and ask His opinion. For that reason, truthfully I find that there are even some G rated movies I shouldn't watch. And, there might be some R rated movies that I should.

That's how God designed it—He doesn't want us living a life in a relationship with the rules. This kind of life really isn't a life at all. Scripture refers to it as bondage! Instead, God redeemed us to live in a relationship with Him, and in that relationship, He will show us what pleases Him and what doesn't please Him. It's also interesting to note, that in that relationship, we won't find ourselves looking around us, but rather acknowledging what God is doing. We'll find ourselves focusing more on Him, not ourselves, and certainly not others.

But you know what? There's more! In addition to not judging one another or forcing one another to live by our own convictions, God instead wants us to help and encourage one another in our walk with Him.

> Let us therefore follow after the things which make for peace and things wherewith we may edify another. (Romans 14:19)
> I THEREFORE, the prisoner of the Lord, beseech you that you walk worthy of the vocation wherewith ye are called, With all lowliness and meekness, with longsuffering, forbearing one another in love; Endeavoring to keep the unity of the Spirit in the bond of peace. (Ephesians 4:1-3)

Most of us are familiar with 1 Corinthians 13, which is usually referred to as the "love chapter." When dealing with our Christian brothers and sisters, it's a chapter we need to return to again and again. I won't repeat it here, but encourage you instead to read it—often! The last sentence of that chapter, however, bears repeating: "…And, the greatest of these is love." (I Corinthians 13:13 NKJV) `

In conclusion, during that period of judging my Christian brothers and sisters, I sure wasn't loving them very much.

Chapter Sixteen

BY WHOSE AUTHORITY?

One of the bigger issues a lot of us face when leaving the LDS church is the issue of authority—Did Jesus give a specific authority to someone, or to a particular group of people, to do His business here on earth? In the LDS church, this issue is very important. Every eligible man has to be ordained by someone else with authority who also was ordained by someone else with authority, right back to Joseph Smith, who claimed to have been ordained by Peter, James, and John. Both the LDS Church and the Catholic Church claim that Jesus directly gave Peter authority when He told him in Matthew 16:

> And I will give unto thee the keys of the kingdom
> of heaven: and whatsoever thou shalt bind on earth
> shall be bound in heaven: and whatsoever thou shalt
> loose on earth shall be loosed in heaven.
> (Matthew 16:19)

Later in Matthew, we read again about the authority Jesus gave the apostles when he sent them out to do His work. They were able to go with His authority and do just what He'd told them to do. We see examples in the book of Acts where Peter raised lepers from their beds, where people were healed just by touching cloths taken from his body, and where he preached in tremendous power too. And, it wasn't just Peter doing these things. Instead, we see all the disciples doing miraculous things through the power of the Holy Spirit. It was truly an amazing time in the life of the church, as the disciples were sent out, literally, into the world and in the power of the Holy Spirit did things they'd never even thought about before.

In Jesus' last command to His disciples we see some hints of why and how His followers would do the things they did.

> And Jesus came and spake unto them, saying, "All power is given unto me in heaven and in earth. Go ye therefore, and teach all nations, baptizing them in the name of the Father, and of the Son, and of the Holy Ghost: Teaching them to observe all things whatsoever I have commanded you: and, lo, I am with you always, even unto the end of the world." Amen. (Matthew 28:18-20)

This command is often referred to as "The Great Commission," and it's included in all four gospels and the book of Acts, so from repetition alone, we infer that it's a very important command. Because it's so important, it's imperative that we understand just what Jesus was commanding. Let's look at a couple more details in that regard:

First, note that Jesus says, "All power is given unto me…," and second, note the very end where He says, "Lo, I am with you always." I point out these passages because I believe these are the keys to knowing and understanding the authority Jesus passed on to His followers to run His church today. First, Jesus has all the power. We don't. Second, Jesus is with us. This implies a living, breathing relationship from which all our own power stems. And, in many ways it's different from what we knew in the LDS church. I imagine you learned like me, that the priesthood (LDS style) was the power to do God's work here on Earth. The priesthood was somehow disconnected from God, and the authority was given to me (well, since I'm a girl, not me exactly but to my husband). It was me, therefore, who had the power and although I was supposed to use it in a right manner and honor God in what I did, it was still me who had the power.

Biblical power, however, is never invested in a man. Instead, it is in God Himself who works His works and His will through man. That's just what we see in the Great Commission—Jesus, who has all the power, is with us doing the work.

In the case of Peter, this was also true. God gave Peter the authority to work in His name, but it wasn't Peter's authority, rather God's authority working through Peter to do His work. Peter understood this. Here's what Peter had to say after a lame man in Acts 3 was healed:

> And when Peter saw it, he answered unto the people,
> "Ye men of Israel, why marvel ye at this? or why look
> ye so earnestly on us, as though by our own power or
> holiness we had made this man to walk?" (Acts 3:12)

Now let's take closer look at what the priesthood is, biblically, to help us gain some insight as to why the biblical priesthood is much, much different from what we learned about in the LDS church.

I'm reading in the end of the book of Exodus right now, and it's quite fascinating (and, yes, sometimes a bit boring) to read the details of how God designed the first tabernacle and dressed

His priests. God appointed Aaron to be the high priest, and in this passage we read how God instructed Aaron, down to the smallest detail of how to make his clothing:

> And these are the garments which they shall make; a breastplate, and an ephod, and a robe, and a broidered coat, a mitre, and a girdle: and they shall make holy garments for Aaron thy brother, and his sons, that he may minister unto me in the priest's office. And they shall take gold, and blue, and purple, and scarlet, and fine linen. And they shall make the ephod of gold, of blue, and of purple, of scarlet, and fine twined linen, with cunning work. It shall have the two shoulder pieces thereof joined at the two edges thereof; and so it shall be joined together. (Exodus 28:4-7)

Continuing through the end of Exodus, the scriptures expand on every little detail about Aaron's clothes, his duties, and what the priesthood meant to Israel.

In the LDS church, we're taught that God set up the Aaronic priesthood for those times to, in essence, run the church. And to some degree, the Levitical line of priests, descendants of Levi, had that job. They were in charge of the tabernacle, later the temple, and everything to do with worshipping in that temple. They killed the animals, they played the music, they performed the sacrifices, they cleaned it, they repaired it, they carried it, and more. In fact, God expressly forbade them to inherit any land as a tribe. Instead, He assigned to them cities and pastures in the midst of the other tribes, because their "inheritance" was in serving God.

Although the priests had the responsibility of caring for the temple, Aaron's descendants didn't have the responsibility of leading Israel.

When Israel demanded a king, for instance, God picked first a descendant of Benjamin, and later descendants of Judah for Kings. He later promised that Judah's descendants would continue as the leaders of Israel forever, which was a prophesy about Jesus who would be the ultimate and final leader of Israel. Note, however, that Jesus Himself is a descendant of Judah—not Levi or Aaron. Before the period of the kings, when God had judges lead Israel, we read about God choosing Othneil of the tribe of Judah, Ehud, a Benjamite, Barak from the tribe of Naphtali, Gideon and Jephthah from the tribe of Manassah, and Samson from the tribe of Dan; I won't go on, but you get the picture. God chose leaders from all, or at least most, of the tribes of Israel to lead the people and did not restrict leadership to the tribe of Levi.

In the Old Testament, prophets weren't necessarily Levites either, which meant they weren't included in the priesthood, because only Levites were allowed to be in the priesthood. Samuel was from the tribe of Ephraim. We don't know for sure which tribe Isaiah belonged to, but since he was of royal upbringing, he probably belonged to the tribe of Judah. Jeremiah, Zechariah, and Ezekiel were Levites. Daniel was a Jew, Jonah a Zebulunite, and the ancestry of the rest of the prophets is unknown.

This observation leads us to believe that in God's plan for mankind, there was no special "group" of people set apart to lead the church, nor was there a special "authority" bestowed on certain people to do God's work, other than the call that God Himself put on their lives. Instead, as we learned earlier, Christ Himself is the head of the church and in a very real sense, each of us "reports" directly to Him. God set up the Old Testament priesthood, though, as a very vivid picture of what He was going to do through Jesus Christ. Studying Jewish traditions with a knowledgeable Christian is very fascinating, because Jewish worship ceremonies and practices all pointed to Jesus.

Hebrews 2 tells us about Jesus and the significance of the priesthood in relation to Him:

> Wherefore in all things it behoved him to be made like unto [his] brethren, that he might be a merciful and faithful high priest in things [pertaining] to God, to make reconciliation for the sins of the people. (Hebrews 2:17)

I mentioned before that God laid out in great detail everything the priests were to do in sacrificing to Him. And indeed we can read all those details in the books of Exodus, Leviticus, Numbers, and Deuteronomy.

But let's focus just a moment on the High Priest's job; Aaron was the first of many.

I mentioned before about Yom Kippur, the Jewish holiday, which literally means the "Day of Atonement." This ritual, too, came from Old Testament times, and here are the exact directions that God gave to Moses for how the priest was to observe this ritual:

> And the LORD said unto Moses, "Speak unto Aaron thy brother, that he come not at all times into the holy place within the veil before the mercy seat, which is upon the ark; that he die not: for I will appear in the cloud upon the mercy seat. Thus shall Aaron come into the holy place: with a young bullock for a sin offering, and a ram for a burnt offering. He shall put on the holy linen coat, and he shall have the linen breeches upon his flesh, and shall be girded with a linen girdle, and with the linen mitre shall he be attired: these are holy garments; therefore shall

he wash his flesh in water, and so put them on. And he shall take of the congregation of the children of Israel two kids of the goats for a sin offering, and one ram for a burnt offering. And Aaron shall offer his bullock of the sin offering, which is for himself, and make an atonement for himself, and for his house. And he shall take the two goats, and present them before the LORD at the door of the tabernacle of the congregation. And Aaron shall cast lots upon the two goats; one lot for the LORD, and the other lot for the scapegoat. And Aaron shall bring the goat upon which the LORD's lot fell, and offer him for a sin offering. But the goat, on which the lot fell to be the scapegoat, shall be presented alive before the LORD, to make an atonement with him, and to let him go for a scapegoat into the wilderness. And Aaron shall bring the bullock of the sin offering, which is for himself, and shall make an atonement for himself, and for his house, and shall kill the bullock of the sin offering which is for himself: And he shall take a censer full of burning coals of fire from off the altar before the LORD, and his hands full of sweet incense beaten small, and bring it within the veil: And he shall put the incense upon the fire before the LORD, that the cloud of the incense may cover the mercy seat that is upon the testimony, that he die not: And he shall take of the blood of the bullock, and sprinkle it with his finger upon the mercy seat eastward; and before the mercy seat shall he sprinkle of the blood with his finger seven times. Then shall he kill the goat of the sin offering, that is for the people, and bring his blood within the veil, and do with that blood as he did with the blood of the bullock, and sprinkle it upon the mercy seat, and before the mercy seat: And he shall make an atonement for the holy place, because of the uncleanness of the children of Israel, and because of their transgressions in all their sins: and so shall he do for the tabernacle of the congregation, that remaineth among them in the midst of their uncleanness. And there shall be no man in the tabernacle of the congregation when he goeth in to make an atonement in the holy place, until he come out, and have made an atonement for himself, and for his household, and for all the congregation of Israel. And he shall go out unto the altar that is before the **LORD**, and make an atonement for it; and shall take of the blood of the bullock, and of the blood of the goat, and put it upon the horns of the altar round about. And he shall sprinkle of the blood upon it with his finger seven times, and cleanse it, and hallow it from the uncleanness of the children of Israel. And when he hath made an end of reconciling the holy place, and the tabernacle of the congregation, and the altar, he shall bring the live goat: And Aaron shall lay both his hands upon the head of the live goat, and confess over him all the iniquities of the children of Israel, and all their transgressions in all their sins, putting them upon the head of the goat, and shall send him away by the hand of a fit man into the wilderness: And the goat shall bear upon him all their iniquities unto a land not inhabited: and he shall let go the goat in the wilderness. And Aaron shall come into the tabernacle of the congregation, and shall put off the linen garments, which he put on when he went into the holy place, and shall leave them there: And he shall wash his flesh with water in the holy place, and put on his garments, and come forth, and offer his burnt offering, and the burnt offering of the people, and make an atonement for himself, and for the people. And the fat of the sin offering shall he burn upon the altar. And he that let go the goat for the scapegoat shall wash his clothes, and bathe his flesh in water, and afterward come into the camp. And the bullock for the sin offering, and the goat for the sin offering, whose blood was brought in to make atonement in the holy place, shall one carry forth without the camp; and they shall burn in the fire their skins, and their flesh, and their dung. And he that burneth them shall wash his clothes, and bathe his flesh in water, and afterward he shall come into the camp. And this shall be a statute for ever unto you: that in the seventh month, on the tenth day of the month, ye shall afflict your souls, and do no work at all, whether it be one of your own country, or a stranger that sojourneth among you: For on that day shall the priest make an atonement for you, to cleanse you, that ye may be clean from all your sins before the **LORD**." (Leviticus 16:2-30)

I've included the entire ritual here because I want you to see for yourself exactly what God instituted. God did this in such great detail because He was painting a picture for us—a picture of what Jesus would do. Here are some highlights:

- This only happened once a year. And it was repeated every year signifying that the blood of the animals didn't fully wash away the sins of the people, but instead had to be applied again and again.
- To start with, the High Priest had to symbolically cleanse himself. The first blood offering was to cleanse himself, then his family and, finally, the people. This process helps us remember that the High Priest, who was a human being, had a sin nature like everyone else. He wasn't separated or higher than others in God's hierarchy, rather he represented them right down to their need to be purified from their sins.
- The High Priest, and only the High Priest, could enter the veil, and he could enter only once a year. Tradition has it, that he wore a rope around his waist to ensure that if something happened, he could be drawn out without someone else entering.
- The entrance to the Holy of Holies was a thick veil—a hands-width thick, which symbolized man's separation from God.
- The blood of the first animal was sprinkled around the altar, cleansing the altar and symbolically all who worshipped there. This ritual was performed because scripture dictated that without the shedding of blood, sins could not be forgiven.

The book of Hebrews lays out in great detail how Jesus fulfilled the prophecy that was given in this ritual. Again and again we're told how Jesus is our high priest, yet He is much more than a High Priest:

> Seeing then that we have a great high priest, that is
> passed into the heavens, Jesus the Son of God, let
> us hold fast our profession. For we have not an high
> priest which cannot be touched with the feeling of
> our infirmities; but was in all points tempted like as
> we are, yet without sin. (Hebrews 4:14-15)

Hebrews chapter 5 tells us that Jesus became a man so that He
could be sympathetic to our weaknesses, just like the Levitical
High Priest could. It also explains how Jesus was called by God
directly to be that high priest just like Aaron was called to be a
High Priest.

> For every high priest taken from among men is or-
> dained for men in things pertaining to God, that he
> may offer both gifts and sacrifices for sins: Who can
> have compassion on the ignorant, and on them that are
> out of the way; for that he himself also is compassed
> with infirmity. And by reason hereof he ought, as for
> the people, so also for himself, to offer for sins. And
> no man taketh this honour unto himself, but he that is
> called of God, as was Aaron. So also Christ glorified
> not himself to be made an high priest; but he that said
> unto him, "Thou art my Son, to day have I begotten
> thee." As he saith also in another place, "Thou art a
> priest for ever after the order of Melchesedec."
> And: Called of God an high priest after the order of
> Melchesedec. (Hebrews 5:1-6, 10)

The comparison in scripture of Jesus to Melchesedec is one
that God makes because Melchesedec in the Old Testament was
a type of Jesus—a picture, if you will—of someone who Abraham gave tithes to. This designation placed Melchesedec at a
higher rank than Abraham. Hebrews 5 shares this. It's a pic-

ture that God shows us to explain that the Levitical priesthood wasn't enough. Instead, the Levitical priesthood would become subordinate to Jesus, because the whole purpose of the Levitical priesthood was to point us to Christ. It's also important to note that, in scripture, there's no indication that Melchesedec held any kind of special power in regard to his priesthood, but instead held a higher rank, or position, than Abraham. Because of that position, Abraham offered tithes to him.

Next, the book of Hebrews tells us that while the High Priests had to make their sacrifices continually year after year for atonement from sin, Jesus made only one sacrifice, and that was all that was necessary to atone the sins of mankind.

> Wherefore he is able also to save them to the uttermost that come unto God by him, seeing he ever liveth to make intercession for them. For such an high priest became us, who is holy, harmless, undefiled, separate from sinners, and made higher than the heavens; Who needeth not daily, as those high priests, to offer up sacrifice, first for his own sins, and then for the people's: for this he did once, when he offered up himself. (Hebrews 7:25-27)

Then, the author of Hebrews takes us back and shows us clearly that while the Old Testament ordinances were for that time, they were no longer needed, because Jesus fulfilled the very thing those Old Testament ordinances pointed to:

> Now when these things were thus ordained, the priests went always into the first tabernacle, accomplishing the service of God. But into the second went the high priest alone once every year, not without blood, which he offered for himself, and for the errors of the people: The Holy Ghost this signifying,

that the way into the holiest of all was not yet made manifest, while as the first tabernacle was yet standing: Which was a figure for the time then present, in which were offered both gifts and sacrifices, that could not make him that did the service perfect, as pertaining to the conscience; Which stood only in meats and drinks, and divers washings, and carnal ordinances, imposed on them until the time of reformation. But Christ being come an high priest of good things to come, by a greater and more perfect tabernacle, not made with hands, that is to say, not of this building; Neither by the blood of goats and calves, but by his own blood he entered in once into the holy place, having obtained eternal redemption for us. (Hebrews 9:6-12)

For Christ is not entered into the holy places made with hands, which are the figures of the true; but into heaven itself, now to appear in the presence of God for us: Nor yet that he should offer himself often, as the high priest entereth into the holy place every year with blood of others; For then must he often have suffered since the foundation of the world: but now once in the end of the world hath he appeared to put away sin by the sacrifice of himself. And as it is appointed unto men once to die, but after this the judgment: So Christ was once offered to bear the sins of many; and unto them that look for him shall he appear the second time without sin unto salvation. (Hebrews 9:24-28)

Finally, Hebrews tells us how we should live now in consequence to what Jesus did:

Now where remission of these is, there is no more offering for sin. Having therefore, brethren, boldness
to enter into the holiest by the blood of Jesus, By a
new and living way, which he hath consecrated for us,
through the veil, that is to say, his flesh; And having an
high priest over the house of God; Let us draw near
with a true heart in full assurance of faith, having our
hearts sprinkled from an evil conscience, and our bodies washed with pure water. (Hebrews 10: 18-22)

When we look at the Old Testament priesthood, we can easily
see that God did not intend it to be an administrative branch
of a church, but rather a picture of what Jesus was coming to
do. The priests painted a picture of our need for a blood sacrifice because we were sinners separated from a Holy God. And,
through the High Priest, depicted a picture of Jesus who would
come and die for us—and once and for all—pay the price for
our sins. Hebrews reiterates that because of Jesus' sacrifice, we
can draw near to God with full assurance, with a confidence, if
you will, that the Israelites never had.

Another symbolic picture God painted for us came when Jesus died
on the cross. Matthew tells us what happened at the moment He died:

And, behold, the veil of the temple was rent in twain
from the top to the bottom; and the earth did quake,
and the rocks rent; (Matthew 27:51).

Remember that the veil of the temple symbolically showed
man that he was separated from God most Holy, or the Holy of
Holies, which was where God symbolically dwelt. Remember,
too, that the veil of the temple was thick cloth. So thick, there
was no way that a man could rip it by himself. But God, to make
the symbolism very clear, ripped the veil from top to bottom!

By Whose Authority?

This miracle shows us that the Holy of Holies, which represents God, is now openly accessible to all through Jesus Christ. Romans 5 mentions that access we have when we place our faith in Jesus Christ.

> Therefore being justified by faith, we have peace with God through our Lord Jesus Christ: By whom also we have access by faith into this grace wherein we stand, and rejoice in hope of the glory of God. (Romans 5:1-2)

As such, the Bible doesn't teach that modern day churches need a priesthood, or a group of men who point toward Jesus. The job that the priesthood represented clearly was completed in Jesus, who now, as our eternal High Priest, stands at the right hand of God making intercession for us. (See Romans 8:34.) Instead, the Bible teaches that all believers have the ability to have a relationship with God without any man coming between them.

Because of what God does in believers through the power of His Holy Spirit, there's no need for someone special to perform certain acts in ministry, such as praying for the sick, picking people for jobs in the church, praying over the communion (or sacrament), leading meetings, or even baptizing. Instead, the Holy Spirit gives gifts to all believers, and in those gifts the church functions. We talked a bit about the gifts the Holy Spirit gives, but let's read about them again:

> Now there are diversities of gifts, but the same Spirit. And there are differences of administrations, but the same Lord. And there are diversities of operations, but it is the same God which worketh all in all. But the manifestation of the Spirit is given to every man to

profit withal. For to one is given by the Spirit the word of wisdom; to another the word of knowledge by the same Spirit; To another faith by the same Spirit; to another the gifts of healing by the same Spirit; To another the working of miracles; to another prophecy; to another discerning of spirits; to another divers kinds of tongues; to another the interpretation of tongues: But all these worketh that one and the selfsame Spirit, dividing to every man severally as he will. For as the body is one, and hath many members, and all the members of that one body, being many, are one body: so also is Christ. (1 Corinthians 12:4-12)

For as we have many members in one body, and all members have not the same office: So we, being many, are one body in Christ, and every one members one of another. Having then gifts differing according to the grace that is given to us, whether prophecy, let us prophesy according to the proportion of faith; Or ministry, let us wait on our ministering: or he that teacheth, on teaching; Or he that exhorteth, on exhortation: he that giveth, let him do it with simplicity; he that ruleth, with diligence; he that sheweth mercy, with cheerfulness. (Romans 12: 4-8)

And he gave some, apostles; and some, prophets; and some, evangelists; and some, pastors and teachers; For the perfecting of the saints, for the work of the ministry, for the edifying of the body of Christ: (Ephesians 4:11-12)

On a practical note, pastors and elders have been gifted by the Holy Spirit and called by God to shepherd, (the biblical meaning of pastor) lead, administer, discern doctrine, and teach. However, their authority to do these jobs clearly comes from the Holy Spirit's gifting just as the person who is given the gift of helps, and performs the more mundane jobs of the church like cleaning up, planning events, or maintenance. Because the Holy Spirit is in charge, however, no special authority is needed for any other believer to pray for each other, administer communion, to baptize, or do whatever else the Holy Spirit tells them to do. Instead, the power and authority comes from Jesus Himself and flows through each of us according to how He wants to use us.

To recap just a bit, the Levitical Priesthood was an organization that God set up to minister to Him in practical ways in temple rituals that pointed to, and painted a picture of, what Jesus would do. When Jesus came to earth, He fulfilled the prophecy this priesthood pointed towards, making it no longer necessary. He was the last, and perfect, High Priest. Because He lives today and sits on God's right hand making intercession for us, there is no need for a human high priest today to continue to make intercession for us.

The priesthood, however, was never about leading an organization, neither the nation of Israel, nor the church, per se. Today, Jesus is the head of the church and has not set up a specific human organization to lead the church. Instead, He works individually with believers, gifting them in certain ways by the Holy Spirit to serve in His church. As believers work together using their gifts and work through their personal relationships with Jesus Christ, the church takes shape with each one serving in his or her gifted area. Some will serve as teachers, teaching, some as pastors, taking care of the flock, some as administrators, administering, some in helps, helping, and more.

The authority to do God's work is invested in every believer as each one steps out into his or her area of gifting under the direction of His leading—God Himself being the one in charge. And that's just what Jesus said when He gave us His last commission. Here it is again to remind you:

> And Jesus came and spake unto them, saying, "All power is given unto me in heaven and in earth. Go ye therefore, and teach all nations, baptizing them in the name of the Father, and of the Son, and of the Holy Ghost: Teaching them to observe all things whatsoever I have commanded you: and, lo, I am with you always, even unto the end of the world." Amen. (Matthew 28:18-20)

So, in conclusion, we see that Jesus is the one who holds the power in the church. He, working through us, gets His job done—whether it's to pray for the sick, lead a church service, appoint new leaders, or do whatever else is needed in the church. Jesus alone was the final and perfect High Priest, and through the work of the Holy Spirit in the lives of believers, directs and leads His church today.

Chapter Seventeen

IF NOT BY FEELINGS,
HOW DO YOU KNOW GOD'S WILL?

Several years ago, my husband and I were presented with an opportunity to do ministry in a way that was somewhat different from what we had been doing. The job offered better pay, benefits (we had none at that point), a house we could live in (saving us the cost of renting), and we'd be doing what we liked, as well as working with people that seemed genuinely nice. Still we agonized over the decision. We prayed, we studied out the scriptures, we talked about it, we made benefits and costs lists, we even got away overnight so that we could really and truly think without the distractions of kids. Finally, we decided to take it, only to quickly change our mind after talking to a few trusted and mature Christians. By then though, we'd already committed to it, and so we had to face the embarrassment of being wrong, frustration from the people we were going to work with and, well, a just plain difficult situation as we backtracked from what we initially thought was the right thing.

But, in that experience, we learned some pretty important principles in determining God's will. Before we go there, however, let's see where we'd been. As LDS folks, we were taught that when the Holy Ghost was talking to us that we'd "feel" His working and know it was God's will, usually with a good feeling or a burning in the bosom. The trouble with that, as we've already explored, is that we also saw, biblically, that our feelings can lead us astray. In fact, we learned that Jeremiah 17:9 tells us that the heart is "deceitful above all things," and therefore we really can't trust what we feel to be right. And in Proverbs 14, we learned that what we think to be right might not be what God sees as "right." Understanding this means that we can't just go by what we see on the surface, such as this job that had some obvious benefits to our family.

We also know, however, that the Christian life is made up of events wherein we experience, or feel, God. And we know that to do that, we need to pray—a lot! In fact, I'd say that we need to pray until we know—really know what it is that God wants us to do. So while we can't do the same things we did when we were LDS to discern God's will, we don't want to totally throw out praying and spiritual feelings. Know, instead, that in addition to praying, we should take some other very important steps when we're attempting to make a decision and want it to be within God's will for us.

First, we need to make sure that our decision is in agreement with God's Word. Remember that the tool God has given us for our sin-tainted decision-making process is God's Word. Throughout scripture we see examples of how to use God's Word in the decision-making process. Psalms 119 likens God's Word to a "lamp" that lights our path. Jesus quoted scripture to

Satan when rebuking him. In fact, Jesus often used scripture to answer people's questions. One example is when the rich young ruler in Luke 18 asked Jesus a question. Jesus answered him by quoting several commandments. The same process applies for us. The first thing we need to do is make sure that whatever we want to do, or not, agrees with what God's written word teaches. If Joseph Smith had done that, for example, he would have known that the angel that came to him couldn't have been from God, since that angel preached a "different gospel." (See Galatians 1.) He also would have "tested the Spirits," (1 John 4:1) and found them to be contrary to God's written word.

In addition to searching God's Word, another biblical principle in seeking God's will is to ask the counsel of trusted and mature Christians. The book of Proverbs tells us:

> Where no counsel is, the people fall: but in the multitude of counsellors there is safety. (Proverbs 11:14)
> The way of a fool is right in his own eyes: but he that hearkeneth unto counsel is wise. (Proverbs 12:15)
> Without counsel purposes are disappointed: but in the multitude of counsellors they are established. (Proverbs 15:22)

It's in our nature to have a tendency to see just what we want to see, and miss really important things. This is just what I did when asking God for an answer to whether the LDS church was true. I wanted it to be true so very badly that my desires made it so I couldn't see, or purposefully ignored, the evidence that the church couldn't be true. James tells us that this is a very real tendency that we humans have:

> Ye lust, and have not: ye kill, and desire to have, and cannot obtain: ye fight and war, yet ye have not,

because ye ask not. Ye ask, and receive not, because
ye ask amiss, that ye may consume it upon your lusts.
(James 4:2-3)

Lust is a real strong word, but remember what we learned
about ourselves? By nature we are lustful people—we want more
than God gives us, whether it be money, possessions, vacations,
a perfect body, beautiful women, handsome men. Whatever it is,
we want more—that's our very nature! I had that brought home
very graphically to me several years ago when we were pretty
tight money-wise. I remember thinking, *If only I could go out to eat,
then I'd be satisfied.* Then my dear husband would come up with
the money to take me out to eat. And guess what? I was satisfied
for about a half hour, and almost immediately after we left the
restaurant, I'd want more. I found myself wanting to do it again,
and again, and again, until I finally realized that going out to eat
wasn't really going to satisfy me at all, and that somehow, and
some way, I had to find my satisfaction in my relationship with
God. Otherwise, I was always going to be lusting after the next
thing that came along.

This is a big topic, and something you might want to keep in
mind as you study things out in your Bible. What's important
to know for now, is that when you talk to, and ask advice of
a trusted and mature Christian, they will be able to see things
that you can't see. They'll be able to judge you from an outsider's perspective, which can then help you to see things from a
less self-centered perspective. In addition, they also might know
something that God's Word has to say about your situation that
you hadn't thought of.

Consider also that it might not just be lust that's keeping us
from seeing clearly. Fear, an incorrect world-view, family pres-

sure, and much more can keep us from seeing a situation clearly. That's why it's a biblical principle to ask advice of godly people as part of our decision-making process.

Lastly, when something is God's will, it will bring peace to us. Whereas Satan has been called "the accuser of the brethren" (see Revelation 12:10), and the father of lies (see John 8:44). Paul taught Timothy that God is not a bringer of discontent, but instead a bringer of peace.

> For God hath not given us the spirit of fear; but of power, and of love, and of a sound mind. (2 Timothy 1:7)

And John told us that God's perfect love will cast our fear from our lives:

> There is no fear in love; but perfect love casteth out fear: because fear hath torment. He that feareth is not made perfect in love. (1 John 4:18)

Peace is another real good indicator that something is from God. In fact, Paul talks to the Philippians about the peace that "passeth understanding" (Philippians 4:7) and that's just what knowing God's will does—it brings you a peace that flies in the face of the facts of your situation. It's the peace of knowing you're in a right relationship with God and doing what He wants, and knowing that because of that, everything else will somehow and someway work out.

That's just what God did in our situation—our embarrassing situation. God took care of every single one of our needs, even though we didn't have super good income, good benefits, or a house paid in full. Instead, God faithfully, month after month, met our needs and gave us a ministry. In that process we grew quite a bit in our relationship with God. We also learned to trust Him and love Him even more, which leads me to my final point. What is God's will?

God's will is that you should grow in your relationship with Him to the point you are "conformed to the image of Jesus," according to Romans 8:29. And subsequently, from that growth, you'll bring Him glory. So, when we're asking God for something, His will is ALWAYS that which would cause us to grow in our relationship with Him. Growing in that relationship isn't always easy or pain-free. In fact, it's sometimes downright painful. This is why James tells us to count it all joy if we go through various problems. James knew that God was using those very troubles to turn believers into the image of Jesus. The same applies to us today (See James 1.)

So, my final step in determining God's will is to check our hearts. We should ask ourselves the following questions:

- Do I want this because it will glorify God?
- Will what I want further or hinder God's kingdom?
- Am I really OK with whatever it is that God wants?
- Am I willing to give up what I want if God wills it?

If we're not there yet, that's okay. Believe it or not, God honors our feelings. He understands them even. But, it's also important that we do some soul searching and be willing to let God truly be the God of our lives. He knows what is best for us, and He wants to work out His perfect will in our lives. But we've got to allow Him to do just that. Sometimes that means we might go through some very hard times. I can't even begin to describe the growth that people I know have experienced in the midst of some truly awful situations.

The important thing to remember is that we're seeking exactly what it is that God has for us—His will in our lives, not our own, and the situation that will bring Him glory. My personal experience with this ministry opportunity is a perfect example. God's answer grew us up a whole lot—but it wasn't the easiest route. It would have been far easier to drift into the job we could have taken. We'd have had better pay, and we'd have had many things that appealed to us at that point in our lives. But what God gave us, by far made up for it—He gave us a better understanding of who He was, and how He works. Job had a similar experience in his book. Maybe you know his story, but God allowed Satan to take away many of the things that brought Job the most pleasure—His children, his wealth, and ultimately, his health. And after Job had gone through this incredible trial, Job makes this statement about God: "I have heard of thee by the hearing of the ear: but *now* mine eye seeth thee." (Job 42:5)

Before the trial, Job knew about God. He knew that God was good and that He was faithful, and I suppose he probably knew many other facts about God because he was a believer. But after Job's trial, he experientially knew God. The same thing was true for my husband and me in our decision. After we'd experienced all the things that God had for us to experience, we, too, could agree with Job and say that we really did "know" God like we hadn't known Him before.

The same will be true for you. If you choose to do whatever it is that God has for you, you will be able to say that you really and truly know God like you hadn't known Him before. And you will realize that knowing God in that way is worth far more than you ever could have imagined.

"For as many of you
as have been baptized into Christ
have put on Christ."

— Galatians 3:27 —

BAPTISM—TO DO
OR NOT TO DO?

When I left the LDS church, I didn't have a clue about biblical Christianity! The only thing I knew is that I loved God and I wanted to serve Him with all that was within me. And, honestly that's not a bad place to be.

Back when my husband and I "walked the aisle," a practice that the Southern Baptist Church used for any time a person wanted to make a decision such as to join the church, believe in Jesus, or commit to some kind of ministry, or even renew their commitment to Jesus, it was explained to me that being re-baptized was the next thing I needed to do.

At that point in my life, my thinking was still very LDS, so I believed that I had to be baptized first as an act of obedience, which would please God in some way, and as the means by which I could join the church. For those reasons, I agreed to be baptized and was baptized two weeks later. However, as I grew in the Lord and came to see just what baptism was all about, I wish I had waited until I really knew what I know now.

Maybe you, too, are a bit confused about this topic. It's another one of those topics that seems to come up a lot for those of us who are ex-Mormons, and you may even have some Christian friends who are putting pressure on you to be re-baptized. For this reason, let's look at baptism more closely and see just what it's all about and why, when, or if we should do it.

Let's start, though, by talking about what baptism isn't.

The first thing we learn about water baptism is that it's not how you join a church. Instead, when you put your faith in Jesus Christ, a spiritual baptism happens. And that baptism puts you into the body of believers, or the church.

The word baptism is often used symbolically in this way. For example, in I Corinthians 10:2, we read about the children of Israel being "baptized" into Moses. In this context, it means to be converted or changed into something, sometimes through hard work, like in the phrase "to go through a baptism of fire."

> For by one Spirit are we all baptized into one body, whether we be Jews or Gentiles, whether we be bond or free; and have been all made to drink into one Spirit. (1 Corinthians 12:13)

In other words, joining the universal church by baptism is not something we do, but instead is something that the Holy Spirit has already done when we put our faith in Jesus. However, we probably will want to join with a local church, and that church will have some kind of process that you'll go through—but it won't usually include baptism, unless you've never had a water baptism before.[1]

Second, baptism isn't about forgiving sins. Scripture is quite clear that believing in Jesus is what gives us forgiveness of sins and it is not something we do. It is only by His grace that we can be forgiven of our sins.

> The God of our fathers raised up Jesus,…for to give
> repentance to Israel, and forgiveness of sins.
> (Acts 5:30-31)
> …In whom we have redemption through his blood,
> the forgiveness of sins, according to the riches of his
> grace; (Ephesians 1:7)
> For by grace are ye saved through faith; and that not
> of yourselves: it is the gift of God: Not of works, lest
> any man should boast. (Ephesians 2:8-9)

Lastly, baptism isn't something we do to merit favor from God, or to help ourselves along on the path to eternal life. Instead, Jesus has already done everything we need to live forever with God the Father.

> According as his divine power hath given unto us all
> things that pertain unto life and godliness, through
> the knowledge of him that hath called us to glory
> and virtue: (2 Peter 1:3)
> And I give unto them eternal life; and they shall never
> perish,… (John 10:28)
> In my Father's house are many mansions: if it were
> not so, I would have told you. I go to prepare a place
> for you. And if I go and prepare a place for you, I
> will come again, and receive you unto myself; that
> where I am, there ye may be also. (John 14:2-3)

What we do see, though, is that full-immersion baptism was a very common practice in the New Testament church. In most cases, it occurred immediately after people put their faith in Jesus. As a pattern, we can see that we too should try to be baptized soon after putting our faith in Jesus Christ as our Savior.

A second important point to remember is that Jesus commanded his followers to baptize the people they converted. This helps
us to know that baptism is something Jesus wants us to do.

> And Jesus came and spake unto them, saying, "All
> power is given unto me in heaven and in earth. Go
> ye therefore, and teach all nations, baptizing them in
> the name of the Father, and of the Son, and of the
> Holy Ghost:" (Matthew 28:18-19)

Sometimes, however, we're faced with what seems to be a par-
adox in scriptures. On the one hand, we know that our salvation
comes by grace, by putting our faith in Jesus. On the other hand,
scripture gives us commandments that we're supposed to follow.
And baptism is one example—it is a work and not necessary for
our salvation, but it's also something we can and should do.

Another thing that really helped me understand a biblical
point of view about baptism was to understand what it really
meant. The Greek word used for baptism is a word that relates
to the process of dying cloth. To baptize cloth meant dipping it
into the dye not just for a short time, but immersing it into the
dye until the dye soaked into the very fibers of the cloth, literally
until there's none of the old color left but the entire cloth right
down to its core was the color of the dye.

The same happens to us when we become Christians. We're
changed completely, right down to our fibers, and instead of being our old selves we become brand new.

> Therefore if any man be in Christ, he is a new crea-
> ture: old things are passed away; behold, all things
> are become new. (2 Corinthians 5:17)

This work, of course, is a work of the Holy Spirit. It's not
something that we can do for ourselves. If it were, I would have

done it for myself a long time ago for sure! Instead, it's the work that God, the Holy Spirit, starts in our lives the moment we put our faith in Jesus. It's also what Jesus was talking about when He was talking to Nicodemus in John 3.

> Jesus answered and said unto him, "Verily, verily, I say unto thee, except a man be born again, he cannot see the kingdom of God." Nicodemus saith unto him, "how can a man be born when he is old? Can he enter the second time into his mother's womb, and be born?" Jesus answered, "Verily, verily, I say unto thee, except a man be born of water and of the Spirit, he cannot enter into the kingdom of God. That which is born of the flesh is flesh; and that which is born of the Spirit is spirit." (John 3:3-6)

Some people take this passage to mean that one has to have a water baptism and a spiritual baptism, but a careful reading of this passage in its context shows clearly that the first birth it's talking about is our physical birth when we were babies. The spiritual birth takes place later when we put our faith in Jesus. Just as we didn't really control our physical birth at all, we can't really control our spiritual birth either—the birth that happens when the Holy Spirit starts His work in our lives and remakes us from the inside out. It's something that happens to us the moment we put our faith in Jesus.

When Jewish proselytes, people who wanted to become Jewish, converted to Judaism, they went through a ceremony where they actually rejected their natural heritage and became Jewish. The completion of this process was a ritual cleaning or bathing. This may be where the idea of baptism originally came from, in fact. Today, when we are baptized, in many ways we are showing the world what God has done inside of us. We're showing how He's taken us out of the family we were born into—the fleshly, sinful family. Remember what Ephesians 2 says about us and who we were before we became a child of God?

> And you hath he quickened, who were dead in trespasses and sins; Wherein in time past ye walked according to the course of this world, according to the prince of the power of the air, the spirit that now worketh in the children of disobedience: Among whom also we all had our conversation in times past in the lusts of our flesh, fulfilling the desires of the flesh and of the mind; and were by nature the children of wrath, even as others. (Ephesians 2:1-3)

Then the scriptures describe how we're brought out of sin and into God's family.

> But God, who is rich in mercy, for his great love wherewith he loved us, Even when we were dead in sins, hath quickened us together with Christ, (by grace ye are saved;) And hath raised us up together, and made us sit together in heavenly places in Christ Jesus: (Ephesians 2:4-6)

That's just what we're showing in a symbolic way when we are baptized into Jesus. We're showing what He's done for us in a very real and graphic way. This symbolic meaning of baptism is what Paul was talking about to the Galatians when he said: " …For as many of you as have been baptized into Christ have put on Christ." (Galatians 3:26-27)

Symbolically, when we are baptized, we show that our old selves have died, and our new selves have resurrected into a new life with Jesus. In Romans 6 Paul talks more about this symbolism when he talks about our spiritual union with Jesus in his death, burial, and resurrection.

> Know ye not, that so many of us as were baptized into Jesus Christ were baptized into his death? Therefore we are buried with him by baptism into death: that like as Christ was raised up from the dead by the glory of the Father, even so we also should walk in newness of life. (Romans 6:3-5)

In this passage Paul shares very graphically the symbolism behind baptism. You see, when we accept Christ, in a very real sense we share His experiences of death, burial, and resurrection. Full immersion baptism symbolizes our death with Christ of our old self, the burial of our old self, and the consequent resurrection we experience when the Holy Spirit makes us into a new man.

Contrary to my baptism, which was only an act of obedience without understanding it, God wants us to understand the relationship He's brought us into, and He wants our baptism to be a celebration of what He's done. It's a public act that demonstrates what He's already done in us. That's exactly why we get baptized.

Because your LDS baptism was about joining a church and making covenants with God, and not about the relationship God has brought you into by His grace, after you've put your faith in Him, I hope you'll decide to be re-baptized when the right time comes. And I pray you do so not because it might be another "work" to check off your to-do list, or because you might be worried about whether God's going to reject you if you don't do it, because He won't. I hope it won't even be because you want to be part of a church, but rather because Jesus has done amazing things in your life and you desire to share that joy with everyone around you by stepping into the waters of baptism.

And would it surprise you to know that I wish I could be there to share it with you? What a party we'd have!

[1]Most Bible-believing churches don't recognize a LDS baptism as a legitimate baptism because a LDS baptism is an work you must do to obtain membership in the LDS church and forgiveness for your sins, rather than a symbolic act showing what Jesus has already done for you on the cross. For that reason most Bible based churches will desire you to be re-baptized at some point in your Christian life.

Chapter Nineteen

PRAISE

Blessed be the God and Father of our Lord Jesus Christ who…. (Ephesians 1:3)
Now unto God and our Father be glory for ever and ever. Amen. (Philippians 4:20)
…Jesus Christ…to whom be honor and power everlasting…. (1 Timothy 6:14-16)
Rejoice in the Lord always: again I will say rejoice! (Philippians 4:4)

Ending anything in life is hard, and transitioning into something new makes it even harder. Leaving Mormonism, as I said before, was the hardest thing I'd ever done in my life. But with that loss came some really neat things. The greatest, and most important, was a relationship with Jesus Christ. What I least expected, though, was praise. Like I've said so often in this book, I can't speak for your experience in Mormonism, but I can speak for mine. My family pattern and my experience with Mormonism was filled with mostly good experiences. My family exemplified the hard working, moral people that Mormonism is known for. They also exemplified a lifestyle that wasn't fully joyful: a lifestyle full of hard work, dedication, and piety. In many ways, there were lots of praiseworthy things in our lives, but no praiseworthy object. Yet the God of the Bible is fully and completely worthy of praise! His works are perfect and wonderful. He Himself is perfect and completely praiseworthy. One thing we see again and again in the Words of His book is the praise that was given to Him throughout the generations.

I bring up this topic because I believe that praise is not natural for those of us who are ex-Mormons. And yet praise is, or should be, an important and intricate part of our Christian life. So I want to close my book with some praise of my own.

You see God's work in my life is an ongoing process. I'm far from perfect, and doubt that I ever will be, but what I do have every single day of my life is the presence of the Risen Savior. He's my closest companion, my dearest friend, and the One who loves me completely and perfectly. He's my Redeemer, my Provider, and my Corrector when I'm wrong.

Not only is He all that, but He's the Creator of the Universe, and not just the Creator, but the One who sustains the universe with the power of His mighty Name. He has my life in His hands and the power to do with it what He wills, yet He chooses to be my closest companion and to richly bless me.

Most of all, God, the God of the Universe, the King of kings, and Lord of Lords chooses me to be His friend. Now that's amazing grace! That's unfailing love!

Know my friend that God desires the same thing for you. He wants to be your companion and friend. He loves you with an everlasting love and wants you to know Him intimately. If you haven't done it yet, can I persuade you to enter that relationship? Truly you'll never regret it!

> O praise the Lord all ye nations, praise Him all ye people, For His merciful kindness is great towards us, and the truth of the Lord endureth forever. Praise ye the Lord. (Psalms 117)

To enter into a relationship with the Creator of the Universe, you simply must put your faith in Jesus—the Jesus of the Bible—and believe that He is able to save you from your sins and redeem you. Putting your faith in Jesus also means that you turn from your past beliefs and sins, and that you forget your past and turn totally towards Him and His truth. This is the biblical meaning of repentance. And that's all that's required biblically. If, however, you'd like to act on this faith right now, you can offer up a simple prayer telling God about your decision. Here's a sample prayer to get you started:

God, I believe that you sent Jesus to die for my sins.
I put my faith in you. I accept You, the God I see in the Bible.
I accept your Son, Jesus, as my Savior.
Forgive me Father for my errors in thinking,
for my stubbornness or ignorance in believing a lie,
and make me Yours forever.
Thank you, God, for taking away my past,
for washing me clean in the blood of Your Son
and not by my own efforts.
Thank you for loving me that much!
I praise your name and give you all the glory.
Amen.

And that's it. You are His, and He is yours!

…In whom we have redemption
through his blood, the forgiveness of sins,
according to the riches of his grace;"
— Ephesians 1:6-7 —